# The Forty Martyrs of England and Wales

## CONTENTS

# Faith and loyalty of the Forty Martyrs of England and Wales - an example to us all

This October marked the 35th anniversary of the canonisation of the Forty Martyrs of England and Wales. Since that period of effective penal law, when being Catholic meant at the least social exclusion and at the most death, several aspects of the Catholic Faith have changed but the fundamentals have remained. For example, as you read this book you will learn that many of the heroic men and women who died for their faith, of whom the 40 are but a few from the hundreds who refused to pray in the vernacular and declined the offer to pray with Protestants, or anyone not of the Catholic Faith.

However, to claim that this is what they died for is wholly wrong. The key point is that they died for supporting the Pope's authority, that notion passed down through generations of apostolic succession. As Cardinal Heenan said at the time of the canonisation: "These men and women gave their lives to defend the truths of the Catholic Faith and the authority of the Vicar of Christ. It is because the Pope's authority is now so often attacked that a reminder of the loyalty of our Catholic fore-fathers is so opportune." It is that fact that is the lasting legacy of the martyrs; despite all the threats and obstacles, they were staunchly loyal to the Church and the Pope, as all Catholics are obliged to be. The martyrs do not belong to any one faction of the Church, traditionalist or liberal, but they belong to all and act as a marker on how to live our faith to its maximum level.

The main source for our biographies was the very rare book *Martyrs of the Catholic Faith* by Bishop Richard Challoner (1691-1781), a copy of which we were very fortunate to discover. It is also from this aged text that much of the Latin spoken by the martyrs is taken, so if it appears 'archaic' – if that is not an oxymoron – then it is because of this. As well as this text, numerous other sources were consulted in an attempt to garner as much information as was possible to fit in the publication. What became clear whilst undertaking this research was the conflicting nature of some of the details about the martyrs, such as different dates here, conflicting stories there. After all, it goes without saying that these were not times to be advertising your activities if you were a Catholic. Thus, the most detailed accounts we have of most of the martyrs surround their trials and deaths, the moments when they were forced into the public's eye and consciousness.

Throughout the publication and the martyrs' tales, we have included other snippets from after their deaths, showing how they have lived on, whether that be the canonisation ceremony itself, old archive photographs of pilgrimages, places you can visit today or relics you can see. By no means have we included every existing link to each of the martyrs but there are enough here to spark an interest and ensure that their legacy and example continues to live on.

# John Houghton O Cart, Tyburn, 1535

From 1523-35 he filled the office of sacristan before becoming procurator from 1528-31. For a few months (June-November 1531), John was prior of Beauvale Charterhouse in Northampton, before becoming prior of the London Charterhouse, just before the storm of the Reformation broke in England.

During this time, John became known for his holiness, love for the Divine Office and reading, self-discipline, and firm but sensible handling of those working under him in the Order. Such qualities saw him also rise to the position of provincial visitor in 1532.

The political and religious landscape changed rapidly in spring 1534, when Henry VIII and Parliament decreed that all men had to take an oath swearing that the king's marriage to Catherine had been invalid and supporting his new one to Anne Boleyn, even though Rome had declared it adulterous. It was known as the Act of Succession, as the oath-taker had to acknowledge that Anne's children would be the rightful and sole heirs to the throne. On behalf of the Carthusian Order, John and the procurator, Humphrey Middlemore, refused to take the oath, leading them to be imprisoned in the Tower of London.

Their ordeal ended when John decided that the addition of the words "so far as it is lawful," meant he could take the oath, albeit with some misgivings, on 29th May, 1534.

Bishop John Fisher and Sir Thomas More, who both later became famous saints, refused even this oath. As a sign of things to come, troops arrived at the Charterhouse in London on 6th April, forcing the other monks to take the oath.

By February 1535 all the loopholes had gone, as Henry and Parliament declared that everyone had to take the Oath of Supremacy, declaring Henry to be the Supreme Head of the Church in England; not to do so was adjudged high treason. This proved to be one step too far for John.

As some other orders and clergy succumbed for various reasons to their temporal ruler's commands, the Carthusian priors of Axholme (in Lincolnshire) and Beauvale (in Nottinghamshire) Charterhouses travelled to London to discuss events with John. They were Augustine Webster and Robert Lawrence respectively.

Following three days of prayer, the three contacted Thomas Cromwell to seek exemption from having to take the oath for themselves and the monks under them. Summoned to take the oath, they flatly refused, having prepared three questions that explained why they could not take it. Stepping forward, John asked Thomas Cromwell how a layman, like the king, could be Christ's vicar. Cromwell's not so witty rejoinder delivered - "You would make the king a priest then?" – he did not wait to hear any more from John, knowing that he was outwitted. Therefore, he promptly had the three brave priors arrested and thrown into the Tower of London, John being incar-

Born in Essex in 1487, John Houghton became the protomartyr of the persecution under Henry VIII and, thus, the protomartyr of the Reformation in England and Wales. Educated at Cambridge University, John graduated with degrees in civil and Canon law in around 1506. His parents, who were minor gentry, then expected him to enter a very good marriage which they had arranged for him. However, John knew that this was not the life for him and, in the end, had to go into hiding to pursue his vocation to the priesthood, lodging with a devout priest who prepared him for ordination.

Once ordained, John served as a parish priest for four years. He soon felt drawn to becoming a Carthusian and entered the Carthusian novitiate in London, where he was professed in about 1516 at the Charterhouse in London.

*continues on page 04*

*"Our Holy Mother the Church has decreed otherwise than the king and parliament have decreed and, therefore, rather than disobey the Church, we are ready to suffer."*

cerated around 13th April, 1535.

Come the trial on 28th April, John stayed true to his Carthusian vow of silence, declining to defend himself in court and refusing to co-operate even by signing. The trial lasted two days, underlining the level of feeling amongst the jury who, despite being ordered to find John and his companions – standing trial together – guilty, refused to do so. Eventually, Cromwell sent a message to them that they would die if they did not find the priors guilty. Still the jury hesitated but a personal visit from Cromwell soon underlined their predicament and they found John and his companions guilty of treason.

The Carthusian priors were to be executed with two others who refused to take the Oath of Supremacy; the Bridgettine monk, Richard Reynolds, and the secular priest, John Hale. Contrary to the custom of the time, all were to die in their clerical clothes. Thus, John Houghton was not stripped of the outward insignia of his faith, as was usual, but instead was prepared for death in his Carthusian habit.

The day of their execution was 4th May, 1535. As they were being prepared for execution, Thomas More was able to watch the group from his cell window in the Tower, noting how they went to their deaths as happily as bridegrooms to a wedding. Each of the condemned were then tied to a hurdle – rectangular frames formerly used as fences or gates which were then dragged through the dirt and the mud behind horses, often suffering terrible injuries dependent on what was littering the road.

Thus, they were taken several miles to Tyburn, where they were to die. John Houghton was the first to suffer whilst the others were forced to watch, in the hope that they would recant, thus discrediting their beliefs and posi- tion. Standing on the cart with the noose above him, John spoke simply and concisely:

"Our Holy Mother the Church has decreed otherwise than the king and parliament have decreed and, there- fore, rather than disobey the Church, we are ready to suffer."

The noose was then placed about his neck, the rope hanging from the infamous triangular Tyburn scaffold, designed in such a shape so that 15 to 20 people could be hanged at once. The cart was then pulled away. This was no mercifully quick snapping of the neck of later years; the rope was already taught before the cart was pulled away, meaning that the prisoner, in this case John, was just left suspended in the air, slowly, agonisingly choking to death.

However, John was cut down whilst still alive. Given a short moment to recover his senses, he was then butchered whilst fully aware of his body being ripped apart by the executioner, trained, as all were, not to cause immediate death by his actions but to keep the subject alive for as long as possible. John's pain was even more excruciating as the executioner had difficulty finding his heart, digging about in the wretched prior's body in an attempt to locate it. Finding the still beating organ, the executioner tore it from John's body and held it aloft, the almost dead John gasping, "Sweet Jesus, what will you do with my heart?" Whether he was still alive to see it thrust into the fire specially prepared is unknown.

The martyr's body was then decapitated and his head displayed on a pike on London Bridge. His quarters were hung at other places, including one, complete with an arm, suspended above the gate of London Charterhouse. The penal era had begun.

*Gate of the London Charterhouse, founded as a Carthusian monastery and dedicated to the Salutation of the Mother of God. The arm of St. John Houghton was hung over the gate after his martyrdom at Tyburn in 1535. Since 1611 it has been Sutton's Hospital in Charterhouse.*

*St. John Houghton (depicted with a swan) presenting the London Martyrs to Our Lady.*

# Richard Reynolds, Brigittine, Tyburn, 1535

After watching the three Carthusian priors viciously being torn apart by the executioner, Richard Reynolds had to witness one more brutal killing before his turn finally came. Richard was the last man to be put to death on that day, after Fr. John Hale, an aged secular priest of Isleworth in Middlesex, who also refused to take the Oath of Supremacy, had been decapitated.

Born in Devon in roughly 1492, Richard studied at Cambridge and was elected a fellow of Corpus Christi College in 1510. After studying to become a Bachelor of Divinity, he was appointed university preacher in 1513 and subsequently was awarded the degree of Doctor of Divinity. That same year, Richard was professed as a Brigittine monk at Syon Abbey in Isleworth, near London. Syon Abbey was the only English house of the Order of St. Saviour, founded by St. Bridget of Sweden in the 14th century. The large building housed both enclosed nuns and priests, such as Richard, all of whom were overseen by an abbess.

Richard quickly developed a reputation as a fearsomely intelligent and deeply devout man. He was considered one of the most outstanding scholars of the day and was reputed to be the only English monk who understood Greek, Latin and Hebrew well. Furthermore, apart from being a famed preacher, his wisdom and holiness were plain for all to see, one contemporary describing him as "a man of angelic countenance, beloved of all and filled with the spirit of God."

When the issues surrounding Henry VIII's divorce and the subsequent Act of Supremacy caused shockwaves around the country, the usual large numbers turned to Richard for advice, including Bishop John Fisher.

Richard did not shirk from his responsibilities and openly preached that the Oath was most definitely against the law of God. For that reason, he refused to take it. Due to his popularity, he was promptly arrested for taking this line, the only one of his community to be so.

In late April 1535, he was brought to trial with the three Carthusians. However, unlike them, he followed no vow of silence so was free to tell the court exactly what he thought. Effectively delivering a ferocious, fiery sermon in court, the judges quickly tried to silence him but not before he had boldly proclaimed, "I have on my side the whole Christian world, except those of this kingdom; nay, I do not say all of this kingdom, for only the lesser part is with you."

Sentenced to the same fate as the others, he was there on the morning of 5th May when Thomas More looked down from his cell and commented on the awaiting condemned to his daughter, Margaret, "Lo, dost thou not see Meg, that these blessed Fathers be now going to their deaths as cheerfully as bridegrooms to their marriage?"

Forced to watch the butchery of the four other martyrs, Richard did not flinch and instead attempted to comfort them through their last painful moments. Having seen the gruesome spectacle, Richard knew what fate awaited him and it was duly carried out. Just as his companions were fully conscious and aware to the end, Richard experienced the same and being dressed in his habit made the acts all the more shocking and despicable to see.

Two weeks later, Henry VIII had Bishop John Fisher's head cut off; two weeks after that, Sir Thomas More suffered the same fate.

Chapter House - English Carthusian Martyrs, St Hugh's Charterhouse

# Augustine Webster O Cart, Tyburn, 1535

The second of the trio of Carthusian martyrs to die on that Spring day in 1535 was Augustine Webster, prior of the Carthusian house near Epworth on the Isle of Axholme in North Lincolnshire since 1531. Formerly a monk of Sheen, like Robert Lawrence, little is known about Augustine. A graduate from Cambridge University, from where he was granted leave to return home for two terms and teach at a grammar school because he had run out of money, Augustine was a Carthusian priest.

Like Robert Lawrence, Augustine arrived in London to discuss with John Houghton the consequences of the announcement of the compulsory Oath of Supremacy. His and the Briggitine, Richard Reynolds' refusal to accept the Act was especially galling for Thomas Cranmer, who had claimed that the Act of Supremacy was necessary "for suppressing the usurped power of the Bishop of Rome."

Writing to Cromwell, Cranmer stated: "I marvel at both, as they are learned men, and Webster promised that he would never support that opinion."

Whether Augustine did ever promise that he would resist any efforts to refuse such an oath is open to question. However, if Augustine had experienced doubts in the past over questions of papal authority against that of a monarch, these were never once in evidence during his interrogations by the royal commissioners. Augustine cited many works in support of the Pope's primacy, including Ss. Jerome, Augustine and Ambrose, resisting with his companions every effort to make him recant and thus discredit his fellow prisoners' beliefs.

Dragged through the backstreets to Tyburn, Augustine was beaten, hanged, drawn and quartered with his fellow Carthusians on 4th May, 1535, fully aware as his intestines were torn from his living body.

Within five years, 18 Carthusians had followed their leaders and had been executed, and every monastery had been dissolved.

Any who, after years of threatened violence, relinquished and then begrudgingly took the oath, later repented their decision.

"I marvel at both, as they are learned men, and Webster promised that he would never support that opinion."

# Robert Lawrence o Cart Tyburn, 1535

Of all the 40 Martyrs, it is one of the earliest who is the least familiar, partly because so little is known about him. We have few facts about Robert Lawrence apart from the details of his death.

Robert's birthplace is even unknown, although it is believed that he could have been from a Dorset family. A Carthusian, he succeeded John Houghton as prior of Beauvale Charterhouse in Nottinghamshire. Previously, it is thought that he may have served as chaplain to the Duke of Norfolk. More certain is that he had spent time as a monk at the London Charterhouse.

However, it was not until February, 1535 that Robert Lawrence stepped into the light of history, although he still remains somewhat shrouded by the mists of time. Returning to his old monastery in London, Robert was seeking a consultation with John Houghton about the desperate situation hanging over the order with the announcement of the Oath of Supremacy. Robert joined in the three days of prayer at the monastery in preparation for the clash that was inevitable.

Robert went with his two Carthusian prior companions, John Houghton and Augustine Webster, to see Thomas Cromwell to explain why they could not take the oath. Thus, the scene was set for him to share in John Houghton's fate; like his companions, paying 6s. 8d. a week for the privilege of being given board and lodging in the Tower of London for the five weeks before their trial; refusing to speak at the trial because of his vow of silence; being dragged though the dirt and baying crowd to Tyburn; watching his friend and religious brother die in the most gruesome manner, knowing that he was to follow.

Whether Robert or Augustine Webster died second – after John Houghton – is unknown, but it is certain that Robert remained staunch in his faith and opinion, despite no doubt being shocked at the sheer brutality with which John Houghton had been dealt. Robert was also cut down from the gallows whilst still fully conscious and aware, so felt every twist of the executioner's knife as his body was ripped apart on 4th May, 1535.

*(left) John Houghton, Robert Lawrence, Augustine Webster and Richard Reynolds before Thomas Cromwell.*

# John Stone OSA, Canterbury, 1539

and to secure the written assent of each community's members to the new order in England. The other houses seemingly went without a murmur but on 14th December, Bishop Ingworth arrived at the Augustinian friary and encountered John Stone.

Presenting himself at the friary, Bishop Ingworth commanded the community to sign the deed of surrender, which would see the king gain ownership of the friary and all its lands. Alone amongst his brothers, John exploded with anger, haranguing the bishop for his servility to the king over God. He outlined his objections to the king's claims to prerogatives that belonged only to the Pope in a succinct manner which left the shocked bishop in no doubt as to the friar's thoughts on the matter. Even as he spoke, the bishop ordered his pikemen to seize John, hoping to separate him from his confreres so that his influence did not spread to them. Hoping to urge John to obey his rule quietly, the bishop sought to convince him to alter his position, in the end even threatening him if he did not do as desired. Bishop Ingworth's shock is evident in the report he wrote to Cromwell:

"Being in the Austin friars there the 14th day of December, one friar there very rudely and traitorously used himself before all the company as by a bill here enclosed you shall perceive part. To write half his words and order there it were too long to write. I, perceiving his demeanour, straight sequestered him so that none spoke with him. I sent for the mayor and ere that he came I examined him before master Spilman and also afterwards before the mayor and master Spilman, and at all times he still held and still desired to die for it, that the king may not be head of the Church of England, but it must be a spiritual father appointed by God."

John persisted in his position, refusing to concede any ground. Thus, he was brought to London, where it was forlornly hoped that Cromwell himself would change the steadfast friar's mind. Despairing, the authorities threw John into the Tower of London, where he lay without charge for a year.

In October, 1539, John was finally sent for his trial, which was to be held at the Guildhall in Canterbury to serve as an example to any others in the city who might be tempted to follow the brave friar's stand. John fasted and prayed solidly for three days whilst awaiting trial in Canterbury Castle. During this time of fasting, John heard a voice calling him by name. Seeing no one, he listened intently to the voice, which bade him to be of good faith, to stand firm and not to hesitate to suffer death for the faith which he professed. From then on, John set forth with renewed strength to never let himself be terrorised into relinquishing his position.

The judges at his trial were the new mayor, Thomas Bele, Sir Christopher Hales and probably Baron John Hales. On 6th December, John was unsurprisingly sentenced to death for high treason and no appeal was per-

Nothing is known of John Stone's early life, except that it was apparently uneventful. It is to be deduced that he was from Canterbury in Kent, for he entered the Augustinian friary there (the friary stood in the area now known as Whitefriars, after the colour of the friars' habits). Leaving to study for a doctorate in divinity at one of the English universities, he was subsequently sent to be professor and later prior at Droitwich. Years later, he was back at Canterbury just as Henry VIII was starting to tear the Church in England in two.

On 3rd November, 1534, the English Parliament issued the Act of Supremacy, which declared Henry VIII as the supreme head of the Church in England. Immediately, John was to be found publicly denouncing this action from the pulpit, as well as announcing his stand on the validity of the monarch's first marriage. He continued ferociously along this track, undeterred by the gradual elimination of all those who criticised the current events in England under the Treason Act, which basically charged anyone who refused to recognise the king as supreme head of the Church with treason.

However, by 1538, Bishop Richard Ingworth, a former Dominican and the official emissary of Thomas Cromwell, who had signed up to the Act of Supremacy and had subsequently been made Bishop of Dover, arrived in Canterbury to close the doors of the mendicant orders

> *"In my death I shall find life, for I die for a holy cause – the defence of the Church of God, infallible and immaculate."*

mitted. His execution was set for two days after Christmas, on the 27th December, and he was sent to Westgate Tower to await his fate.

When the day of his execution came, John remained steadfast. Highlighting to the people that he was an exceptional 'criminal', the execution took place just outside the city at a specially built gallows on a prominent hill known as Dane John. Dragged on a hurdle from Westgate Tower to the spot of execution, John suffered the unhappy experience, as the noose tightened around his neck, of being able to see his friary from the vantage point of the hill, the building already stripped of its former past and glories. As the executioners were preparing the apparatus for his death before his very eyes, John announced to the gathered crowd, "Behold, I close my apostolate in my blood. In my death I shall find life, for I die for a holy cause – the defence of the Church of God, infallible and immaculate." The stalwart friar was then hanged, drawn and quartered. His head and quarters were exhibited at the city gates, serving as a warning to any Catholics living in the city.

*The Dane John, Canterbury, where St. John Stone was martyred.*

# Cuthbert Mayne, priest, Launceston, 1577

Cuthbert Mayne was the first missionary priest of the period to suffer death. He was born at Youlston, three miles from Barnstaple in Devonshire in roughly 1544 (baptised 20th March, 1544). His uncle was a Protestant minister and was eager to leave his ample benefice to his nephew. Therefore, he ensured Cuthbert was well educated at Barnstaple Grammar and when he was 18 or 19, had him made a minister. Unaware of the different religions, Cuthbert complied and went to St. Alban's Hall, Oxford, where he became a Bachelor of Arts and made the acquaintance of a series of later-famous Catholics including Edmund Campion, Gregory Martin and Henry Shaw to name but a few.

At the time, St. John's College was looking for a Fellow of the University to become the college chaplain. He held this position for many years and was greatly loved by the Protestants but pitied by the Catholics. The latter regularly advised him of the sin in which he was living and Cuthbert took heed of their warnings, realising that this 'new doctrine' was heretical. Deploring the state he found himself in, Cuthbert became Catholic in mind but still continued in the same college for several years, becoming a Master of Arts.

However, he regularly received letters from his friends, Edmund Campion and Gregory Martin, urging him to leave the ministry and join them across the seas. One of these letters, from Gregory Martin, fell into the hands of the Bishop of London, who immediately dispatched some guards straight to Oxford to seize Cuthbert and some others. Luckily, Cuthbert had returned home at the time. Being warned of the plot to arrest him by his friend Thomas Ford (a Fellow of Trinity College, Oxford, and later a martyr), Cuthbert escaped by a boat off the coast of Cornwall and went to Douai, where the seminary had just been established.

Arriving in Douai in 1573, he was reconciled to the Church and began his training to become a priest. Completing his studies in Divinity, he was ordained in 1575. Moved partly by awareness that his former sacrilegious service had offended God, and partly by a zeal to save souls, he returned to England. Dr. William Allen, later Cardinal and first President of the College, sent him to his homeland with John Payne and Henry Shaw on 24th April, 1576. Cuthbert returned to the southwest and stayed with a Catholic and virtuous gentleman called Francis Tregian, who lived in Golden, just outside Truro, Cornwall. For disguise, the priest pretended to be Tregian's steward.

In June 1577, the Bishop of Exeter was visiting Truro and was requested by Richard Grenville, the Sheriff of the County, to assist in a search of Tregian's house. After some deliberation, it was decided that the Sheriff, along with the Bishop's Chancellor and various others, would see to the matter. Coming to the house on 8th June, the Sheriff informed Tregian that they were going to search his property for a man called Bourne, who had committed a crime in London and had sought refuge in this house according to an informant. Tregian swore that he did not know where this man was and thought it was a disgrace that they planned to search his house, that of a gentleman, without a commission from the Queen. Being emboldened by the support around him, the Sheriff swore that he would search the house, even if it meant him being killed or having to kill. With that, he grabbed his dagger and pointed it at Tregian's chest.

Fearfully, Tregian relented and the search group entered the building. They immediately went to Cuthbert's room and, finding the door bolted they began to batter it down. Hearing the commotion, Cuthbert came from the garden to open it for them. As soon as the Sheriff entered the room, he grabbed a handful of the priest's shirt and demanded, "What art thou?" Answering that he was a man, the sheriff, pounding on adrenaline, ordered Cuthbert to remove the coat of mail under his doublet. The offending item unbuttoned, the Sheriff discovered an *Agnus Dei* case (a small plaster disc embossed with the figure of the Lamb of God) around Cuthbert's neck. Seeing it, the Sheriff denounced him as a traitor and a rebel and began to shout abuse at him. Thus, Cuthbert Mayne was arrested on 8th June, 1577.

Seizing Cuthbert, they carried him, his books, papers and letters to the Bishop of Exeter. After being examined by the bishop, who found him a very learned man, Cuthbert was brought to various gentlemen's houses, till he came to Launceston. Here, he was cruelly imprisoned, being chained to his bed with a pair of great shackles around his legs. Moreover, no one was allowed to talk to him.

He remained in this state from June until Michaelmas, at which time the judges arrived on their circuit. The Earl of Bedford led the proceedings against the captured priest, who was charged with five offences. Firstly, he was charged with obtaining a Papal Bull, containing details of absolution to the queen's subjects. Secondly, this Bull had been published at the house of Tregian. Thirdly, Cuthbert had maintained the usurped power of the Pope, thus denying the Queen's supremacy. Fourthly, he had brought an Agnus Dei into the kingdom and delivered it to Tregian. Lastly, he had said Mass at Tregian's house.

There was not sufficient proof for any of these charges. For example, the alleged Papal Bull was only a printed copy of an out-of-date jubilee indulgence bought as a curio in Douai, so not from Rome or Tregian's house. Yet

Judge Manhood, who behaved in an improper manner throughout the proceedings, advised the jury to find him guilty, advising that where plain proofs were lacking, strong presumptions would be enough. Thus, according to his logic, they had strong presumptions that he was guilty because he was a priest and so an enemy of the queen's religion.

The jury was also rigged to ensure the result; the members' staunch Protestant values would find him guilty of everything just because he was a priest. However, even they were more than a little sceptical about the evidence presented to them but any indecision was quickly allayed after Sheriff Grenville had harangued and threatened them. Duly found guilty, Cuthbert was sentenced to death for high treason by Judge Manhood. Keeping calm and relatively cheerful, Cuthbert lifted his hands and eyes to heaven, proclaiming, *Deo gratias* ("Thanks be to God"). Originally, he was to be executed 15 days after the trial but it was deferred till St. Andrew's Day. The reason for the delay is thought to be that Judge Jeffreys heard about the despicable proceedings and informed the Privy Council. Thus, it was decided that all the judges would meet to discuss the matter. However, despite several older and wiser judges agreeing with Jeffreys' sentiments, the Privy Council maintained that Cuthbert should still be executed as a warning to other Catholics. Furthermore, it was also decreed that Cuthbert should be executed in the market square on market day to ensure that the message was driven home to all Catholics in the area. The Sheriff who procured the death warrant at the meeting was the same man who had arrested the condemned priest; he was knighted for his service in the cause.

Three days before his execution, Cuthbert was advised to prepare for death by a serving-man. The priest kindly thanked the man and said that if he had anything to give, he would rather bestow it upon him for he had done more for him than any man ever did. Finally knowing for certain his hour of death, Cuthbert devoted himself to prayer and contemplation. On the second night (27th November) of these exercises, his cell was filled with a bright light between midnight and one o'clock in the morning, prompting many of the other prisoners to call out; they could not understand the source of the light for they knew he had no candle.

On the day of his execution, many justices and gentlemen came to see him, along with two ministers. They disputed with him about religion but Cuthbert outwitted them on every level. The onlookers resorted to claims that the ministers were far better educated than him. They then offered Cuthbert his life if he would renounce the Catholic faith. When he refused, they urged him to at least swear on the Bible that the queen was the supreme head of the Church of England, once again assuring him of his life if he did so. Taking the Bible and making the Sign of the Cross upon it, he kissed it before proclaiming "The queen neither ever was, nor is, nor ever shall be, the head of the Church of England." Infuriated, the group left him be.

Cuthbert was to be drawn a quarter of a mile to the place of execution. When he came to his sledge, some of the crowd, still peeved at the priest's earlier display, asked that his head be placed over the edge of the sledge so that it would scrape all the way along the ground. Cuthbert himself offered to accept the punishment but the Sheriff's deputy refused.

Arriving at the unusually tall gibbet that had been erected for his death in the marketplace, the condemned priest knelt down and prayed. Once he had mounted the ladder and had the rope placed round his neck, he turned to address the crowd but was forbidden to speak by the justices, who advised him to say his prayers. This he did devoutly.

The hangman was about to remove the ladder when one of the justices spoke to Cuthbert:

"Now, villain and traitor, thou knowest that thou shalt die, and therefore tell us whether Mr. Tregian and Sir John Arundel did know of these things which thou art condemned for, and also what thou dost know by them?"

Cuthbert retorted mildly: "I know nothing of Mr. Tregian and Sir John Arundel, but that they are good and godly gentlemen; and as for the things I am condemned for, they were only known to me, and to no other."

With that, he was pushed off the ladder, beating his breast and uttering the words, *"In manus tuas..."*

Some spectators called for him to be cut down straight away so that he could be quartered alive. However, the Sheriff's deputy refused their bloodthirsty cries and let Cuthbert hang until he was almost dead. When he was cut down, the size of the gibbet was so large that he fell a great height, smashing his face on the side of the table on which he was to be butchered. Therefore, he was thankfully not fully aware of the torture subsequently inflicted upon him, the executioner stripping the priest of his clothes before slitting open his stomach, tearing up his intestines and finally brandishing Cuthbert's heart as some form of trophy. His quarters were disposed to Bodwin, Tregny, Barnstaple and Launceston Castle. His head was set on a pole on a busy road at Wadebridge.

The hangman who had tortured the heroic priest so mercilessly went mad within a month of the martyrdom, and died miserably soon after. It is also remarked that not one of those Cuthbert reconciled to the Catholic Church could ever be induced to renounce their faith, which they had learnt in depth from their good master. However, Tregian lost his considerable estate and was condemned to life imprisonment. Several of his neighbours were also imprisoned as accomplices of the martyred priest, as well as Sir John Arundel, who was continually persecuted.

*Cuthbert Mayne suffered at Launceston, Cornwall on 29th November, 1577.*

# Edmund Campion SJ, Tyburn, 1581

Edmund Campion was born in London on 25th January, 1540. After receiving his initial education at Christ's College on Newgate Street, London (where his outstanding gifts of oratory were already evident and led to him being chosen to welcome Queen Mary on her entrance into the city), he attended the newly founded St. John's College, Oxford. By the age of 17, he was already a fellow of the university. Here, his academic excellence won him much admiration from the college's founder, Sir Thomas White. Thus, Edmund gave an oration in Latin at the founder's funeral, having previously given one in English at that of Lady Dudley, late wife of the Earl of Leicester, despite being a layman. Six years after welcoming Queen Mary, Edmund welcomed another queen, this time Elizabeth, to the university. Taking part in a debate infront of the monarch, Edmund so impressed Elizabeth, that she requested he give a repeat performance at Woodstock.

Having completed his time at Oxford with great success, his friends persuaded him to become a Protestant deacon, seeing it as further 'promotion' for him. However, whilst serving in this capacity, Edmund's ambition began to waver and he started to realise his Catholic inclinations. After spending some more time in study, he travelled to Ireland, a country whose history he wrote, not without controversy.

Soon, Edmund heard that a seminary had opened in Douai and decided to go there himself. Robert Cecil, one of the Queen's most trusted advisors, on hearing of Edmund's conversion to Catholicism and leaving of England, commented that, "England has lost one of her diamonds." Under the guidance of the college's founder, Dr. William Allen, Edmund studied the Catholic faith diligently. In time, he became a Bachelor of Divinity. Nevertheless, he still could not rid himself of the feeling of sin surrounding his deaconship, made even more pointed now that his studies had led to an increased devotion, zeal, learning and judgment. In time, he realised the only way to rid himself of this sin was a penance as great as becoming a priest.

Thus, he chose to join the Society of Jesus and become a Jesuit. He has been regarded as one of the Society's greatest members ever since. Heading to Rome, he was admitted by the General of the Order in April, 1573, and after a month in the city, was sent to Bohemia. He stayed in Prague for seven years (ordained in 1578), continually teaching, preaching, catechising, writing and labouring for the Church. Edmund's intelligence quickly brought him great fame, and various principal state leaders, including the Imperial Majesty himself, often desired to hear him preach. Furthermore, he received a vision of his own martyrdom from Our Lady whilst sitting in a garden in Brunn.

Such fame and notoriety for achieving conversions did not escape the notice of the General of the Order. He decided to send Edmund on the mission to England. Stopping at Rheims (where the College of Douai was by then situated), he met another fabled Jesuit – Fr. Robert Parsons. Whilst there, Edmund visited the principal, Dr. William Allen, and asked him if all the troubles that he would have to overcome, and the gap he had left in Prague, were worth the successes he may be able to achieve in England. Dr. Allen replied as follows:

"Father, whatever you did there [Prague] may be done by others, one or more of your order. Secondly, you owe more duty to England than to Bohemia, and to London than to Prague; though I am glad you have made some recompense to that country for the old wound it received from us in Wycliffe's time, from whom the Hussites of Bohemia learned their heresies. Thirdly, the recovery of one soul from heresy is worth all your pains, as I hope you will gain many, because the harvest is both more plentiful and more ripe with us than in those parts. Finally, the reward may be greater; for you may be martyred for it at home, which you cannot easily obtain there."

Such an answer satisfied Edmund and he was known to often mention it in conversation. On his way back to England, he reportedly stopped off at Geneva, where he challenged Calvin's successor, Dr. Beza, to a public debate. He landed at Dover the day after Midsummer, 1580, somehow escaping the coastguards who detained him for several hours whilst they deliberated whether to send him to the Privy Council.

Arriving in London, he preached his first sermon on the feast of Ss. Peter and Paul in front of a huge crowd. Persons of distinction regularly came to hear him preach. As his fame grew and news of his virtues, eloquence and learning spread, many Protestants came to hear him and forever afterwards unfavourably compared their own preachers to this superb orator.

He always preached at least once, often twice, and sometimes even three times a day. Through this preaching, he succeeded in converting a sizeable number of people in most of the counties of England, ranging from high-ranking men to students and all other social levels. Edmund soon realised that his preaching was a great success and so wrote to the head of the Society of Jesus, Everardus Mercurianus, advising him that those sent to England should be excellent preachers. In the same letter, he acknowledged the good work done for him and the Society by the missionaries of the secular clergy, who had been 'keeping' the country for many years before his arrival.

At the same time, Edmund sent some writings to the Universities of Cambridge and Oxford. The Protestant preachers and prelates of the universities, deeply stung by his eloquent attacks, launched a number of pamphlets against him. More threateningly, they advised the Privy Council to see the controversies as being aimed at the queen, so were matters of State, rather than religion. Not able to battle Edmund with their inferior learning in matters of divinity, they thus

sought to silence him by force.

Therefore, many speeches were given and proclamations made alleging that the Pope, in alliance with various Catholic rulers, planned to invade England, and that the Jesuits and seminary priests had been sent to prepare the way. Similar claims were made to rouse the population against the mission; all efforts were centred on apprehending these priests, and specific attention placed on Edmund, who they labeled "the Pope's Champion".

After 13 months of being constantly hunted in England, Edmund Campion was betrayed by the notorious priest catcher, George Eliot. On 17th July,

1581, the Jesuit was found hiding in a priest hole at Lyford Grange, near Abingdon in Berkshire, home of the Catholic gentleman, Mr. Yates. Edmund's stirring booklet, entitled *Ten Reasons*, had caused outrage amongst the authorities. Known as 'Campion's Brag' it had been written as an open letter to the Privy Council to present his case if he was captured, but was printed prematurely, addressing Elizabeth on the certain triumph of Catholicism – "The expense is reckoned, the enterprise is begun. It is of God, it cannot be withstood. So the Faith was planted, so it must be restored." Given refuge at Stonor Park, it was there that Campion

wrote his 'Brag', thought to be one of the earliest defences of Catholicism in English during the Reformation. The rousing text ran as follows:

"To the Right Honourable, the Lords of Her Majesty's Privy Council:

"Whereas I have come out of Germany and Bohemia, being sent by my superiors, and adventured myself into this noble realm, my dear country, for the glory of God and benefit of souls, I thought it like enough that, in this busy, watchful, and suspicious world, I should either sooner or later be intercepted and stopped of my course.

"Wherefore, providing for all events, and uncertain what may become of me, when God shall haply deliver my body into durance, I supposed it needful to put this in writing in a readiness, desiring your good lordships to give it your reading, for to know my cause. This doing, I trust I shall ease you of some labour. For that which otherwise you must have sought for by practice of wit, I do now lay into your hands by plain confession. And to the intent that the whole matter may be conceived in order, and so the better both understood and remembered, I make thereof these nine points or articles, directly, truly and resolutely opening my full enterprise and purpose.

**i.** I confess that I am (albeit unworthy) a priest of the Catholic Church, and through the great mercy of God vowed now these eight years into the religion [religious order] of the Society of Jesus. Hereby I have taken upon me a special kind of warfare under the banner of obedience, and also resigned all my interest or possibility of wealth, honour, pleasure, and other worldly felicity.

**ii.** At the voice of our General, which is to me a warrant from heaven and oracle of Christ, I took my voyage from Prague to Rome (where our General Father is always resident) and from Rome to England, as I might and would have done joyously into any part of Christendom or Heatheness, had I been thereto assigned.

**iii.** My charge is, of free cost to preach the Gospel, to minister the Sacraments, to instruct the simple, to

*continues on page 14*

reform sinners, to confute errors—in brief, to cry alarm spiritual against foul vice and proud ignorance, wherewith many of my dear countrymen are abused.

**iv.** I never had mind, and am strictly forbidden by our Father that sent me, to deal in any respect with matter of state or policy of this realm, as things which appertain not to my vocation, and from which I gladly restrain and sequester my thoughts.

**v.** I do ask, to the glory of God, with all humility, and under your correction, three sorts of indifferent and quiet audiences: the first, before your Honours, wherein I will discourse of religion, so far as it toucheth the common weal and your nobilities: the second, whereof I make more account, before the Doctors and Masters and chosen men of both universities, wherein I undertake to avow the faith of our Catholic Church by proofs innumerable—Scriptures, councils, Fathers, history, natural and moral reasons: the third, before the lawyers, spiritual and temporal, wherein I will justify the said faith by the common wisdom of the laws standing yet in force and practice.

**vi.** I would be loath to speak anything that might sound of any insolent brag or challenge, especially being now as a dead man to this world and willing to put my head under every man's foot, and to kiss the ground they tread upon. Yet I have such courage in avouching the majesty of Jesus my King, and such affiance in his gracious favour, and such assurance in my quarrel, and my evidence so impregnable, and because I know perfectly that no one Protestant, nor all the Protestants living, nor any sect of our adversaries (howsoever they face men down in pulpits, and overrule us in their kingdom of grammarians and unlearned ears) can maintain their doctrine in disputation. I am to sue most humbly and instantly for combat with all and every of them, and the most principal that may be found: protesting that in this trial the better furnished they come, the better welcome they shall be.

**vii.** And because it hath pleased God to enrich the Queen my Sovereign Lady with notable gifts of nature, learning, and princely education, I do verily trust that if her Highness would vouchsafe her royal person and good attention to such a conference as, in the second part of my fifth article I have motioned, or to a few sermons, which in her or your hearing I am to utter such manifest and fair light by good method and plain dealing may be cast upon these controversies, that possibly her zeal of truth and love of her people shall incline her noble Grace to disfavour some proceedings hurtful to the realm, and procure towards us oppressed more equity.

**viii.** Moreover I doubt not but you, her Highness' Council, being of such wisdom and discreet in cases most important, when you shall have heard these questions of religion opened faithfully, which many times by our adversaries are huddled up and confounded, will see upon what substantial grounds our Catholic Faith is builded, how feeble that side is which by sway of the time prevaileth against us, and so at last for your own souls, and for many thousand souls that depend upon your government, will discountenance error when it is bewrayed [revealed], and hearken to those who would spend the best blood in their bodies for your salvation. Many inno-

*Mass is offered, July 1970, outside Lyford Grange, the house where St. Edmund Campion was captured.*

cent hands are lifted up to heaven for you daily by those English students, whose posterity shall never die, which beyond seas, gathering virtue and sufficient knowledge for the purpose, are determined never to give you over, but either to win you heaven, or to die upon your pikes. And touching our Society, be it known to you that we have made a league - all the Jesuits in the world, whose succession and multitude must overreach all the practice of England - cheerfully to carry the cross you shall lay upon us, and never to despair your recovery, while we have a man left to enjoy your Tyburn, or to be racked with your torments, or consumed with your prisons. The expense is reckoned, the enterprise is begun; it is of God; it cannot be withstood. So the faith was planted: So it must be restored.

**ix.** If these my offers be refused, and my endeavours can take no place, and I, having run thousands of miles to do you good, shall be rewarded with rigour. I have no more to say but to recommend your case and mine to Almighty God, the Searcher of Hearts, who send us his grace, and see us at accord before the day of payment, to the end we may at last be friends in heaven, when all injuries shall be forgotten."

ered, Frs. Ford and Collington. The three priests were found lying on a specially made-up bed in the hiding place, all praying at the time of their discovery. Before being captured, Edmund had offered to give himself up to avoid any hardship for the family and those present at the house. However, they would not allow it, so he and the other two priests heard each other's confessions before praying that God's will be done.

"Thy will be done, O Lord! St. John Baptist, pray for me!"

John the Baptist was Edmund's favoured saint. He believed that the blessed saint had interceded on his behalf to help him escape his captors at Dover.

Now in the hands of Eliot and the guards, his enemies, Edmund was abused and mocked. However, he remained calm, and such was his remarkable modesty, mildness and humility that he set a great example to Catholics and left his enemies astonished. After spending two days in the custody of the Sheriff of Berkshire, he was taken, along with all those captured in the raid, to London. On the way to the city, many scholars from Oxford University came to see this famous man at Abingdon, and Edmund offered to preach for them.

There, at dinner, Eliot lamented to the priest that he looked kindly upon everyone except him: "I know you are angry with me in your heart for this work."

Edmund responded: "God forgive thee, Eliot, for so judging of me. I forgive thee, and in token thereof I drink to thee. Yea, and if thou wilt repent and come to confession, I will absolve thee; but large penance thou must have."

On the journey to London, they tied Edmund's legs under his horse, bound his hands, and the Privy Council ordered that a piece of paper be stuck on his hat that read in large capital letters, 'CAMPION THE SEDITIOUS JESUIT'. Moreover, orders were given to stay at Colebrook on Friday so that Edmund and his companions could be marched through London in triumph on the Saturday. This was a market day in many places, so the route would be thronged with the very people in which the Council sought to arouse hatred.

Almost all of London saw the spectacle on 22nd July. The mob delighted in the novelty but the wise mourned the country's fall to such barbarity, where it was game to abuse a religious man, honoured in so many other nations for his learning, and innocent of any crime. He was then delivered to the Lieutenant of the Tower.

The Lieutenant's deep loathing of Catholics exacerbated the miseries of the Tower. After a number of examinations and threats by the Lord Chancellor and others of the Privy Council, Edmund was racked several times. His torturers hoped to discover whose houses he had frequented; who had helped him; who he had reconciled and when; for what purpose had he reconciled them; when had he entered the country and on what commission; and who printed and distributed his books.

After his first racking, it was clear that Edmund would reveal nothing, nor compromise his religion in any way. Thus, they decided to invent accusations of treason against him. It was on these charges that he was so mercilessly torn apart by the rack on two more occasions, leading him to confide in a friend that he thought they were going to kill him in this manner. Before entering the torture room, Edmund would fall to his knees, commending himself to God's mercy, whilst he continually called on God and Jesus during his tortures. However, he still managed to forgive his torturers and those who laid the false charges against him.

The racking was severe. When asked by his jailer how his hands and feet felt, Edmund commented that they did not feel sore because he could not even feel them at all. This result did not satisfy his torturers though, and they inflicted much more on his body in secret. Furthermore, they invented more fabrications to slander his name in public, urging the Protestant preachers to denounce him from their pulpits. They even published reports claiming that he would convert to Protestantism, or that he had already conformed. Rumours were spread that he had confessed all he knew whilst on the rack and had then committed suicide in his cell. No

Travelling north, Edmund had stopped at Lyford Grange by request. However, after Eliot had betrayed him, 100 men appeared at the house, ransacking it in an attempt to find the hidden priest and prize capture. Before making his escape, those at the house urged Edmund to give a final sermon, which he duly did at the dead of night, whilst the hunters slept downstairs. The 'congregation', delighted after hearing the great man speak one last time, began to head quietly to bed but, disastrously, one tripped in the dark, creating a deafening commotion as the others fell over him. This calamity woke the guards and led to the capture of the fabled Jesuit that night, despite his managing to return to the priest hole in which he had been hiding.

Two other priests were also discov-

*continues on page 16*

doubt this last rumour is what would have been claimed had the racking actually killed him, as it so nearly did.

The Lieutenant of the Tower at first tried to convince Edmund to convert, using promises and threats to urge his conformity. For example, he claimed that the Jesuit was one of the greatest men England had ever produced, and God had brought him home to England so that he could bring glory to the queen. Sometimes he met privately with Edmund, urging him to display just some small indication of conformity. When this failed, public disputes were set up against supposedly learned Protestant ministers. Here they would berate Edmund, goading him incessantly, this poor man, nearly racked to death. However, when Edmund tried to respond to their barbed insults, he was threatened to silence by the presiding authorities with laws and punishment. They disputed with him in this manner three times, showing little but contempt and malice for the great man, whilst demonstrating a deep ignorance in divinity, causing embarrassment to a number of Protestants who marvelled at the learning and humility of the priest. However, he bravely remained undefeated, particularly impressing the watching Philip Howard, Earl of Arundel.

With it becoming clear that Edmund would not falter in any way, his enemies began to devise a show of justice that would charge him and his companions with treason against the queen and the state. For this purpose, they found three or four infamous liars who would not hesitate to swear against a man they had never met or seen before his London 'parade'. Thus, an indictment was drawn up against him and a number of other priests of which the jury (deeply biased by fear and authority) could not help but find them guilty.

On 14th November, 1581, he and seven others were brought from the Tower to the King's Bench bar at Westminster Hall. The seven arraigned with Edmund were Ralph Sherwin, Luke Kirby, Thomas Cottam, Robert Johnson and Edward Rishton, all of whom were priests from Douai College; James Bosgrave, a young Jesuit, who had come over to England in the hope of improving his health; and Mr. Orton, a layman. A charge was read to them claiming that in the 22nd year of the queen's reign, on the last day of May whilst on the continent, they had plotted the queen's murder, rebellion within the country and invasion from without. Edmund was ordered, with the others, to hold up his hand and make his plea, as was the custom in such cases. However, his arm being crippled from the tortures he had already endured and wrapped in a furred cuff, Edmund could not comply. Thus, one of his companions, kissing the abused hand, took off the pitiful priest's cuff and defiantly lifted the arm as high as he could so that Edmund could plead not guilty with the rest:

"I protest before God and His holy angels, before heaven and earth, before the world and this bar whereat I stand, which is but a small resemblance of the terrible judgment of the next life, that I am not guilty of any part of the treason contained in the indictment, or of any other treason whatsoever. Is it possible to find 12 men so wicked and void of all conscience in this city or land that will find us guilty together of this one crime, divers of us never meeting, or knowing one the other, before our bringing to this bar?"

Nothing else was done that day but a trial set for 20th November. The jury was chosen, but on the day three of them did not appear, knowing that justice would not be done because of the thirst for blood.

In the meantime, Edmund and the other priests were taken back to the prison from whence they had come. The next day, the following were arraigned in a similar manner: John Collington or Colleton, Laurence Richardson, John Hart, Thomas Ford, William Filby and Alexander Briant, all priests from Douai; and John Shert, also a priest, but ordained in Rome.

On 20th November, Edmund and his companions were returned to the court to receive judgment. A huge crowd of people gathered to see the events, many of them honourable and learned gentlemen keen to see if England's world famous law could stand its ground against the violent impression of power and authority with which it was threatened. Some came to witness the end of this gruesome tragedy that contained various acts of examining, racking, disputes and torture. Others came to see if there were any men left who would risk their office and lives rather than condemn men they knew to be innocent. However, this sad day only gave witness to the sullying of the law and the fall of the Catholic Church in England.

Nothing the queen's attorney, lawyer, counsellors or witnesses of the racking said could prove the guilt of the accused. Nor could the false witnesses, Eliot, Cradock, Sled and Munday, prove to any semi-intelligent person that these men were guilty. Point by point, the accused, particularly Fr. Campion, disproved the presented evidence. His innocence especially was obvious to all; in fact, it was so blatant that when the jury retired to decide its verdict, many learned men and renowned lawyers concluded that in no way could Edmund be pronounced guilty.

However, the authorities wanted Edmund dead and nothing could save him or the others. The jury did what Mr. Popham, the Attorney-general, advised them was the queen's will, and pronounced them guilty. All the men were sentenced to be hanged, drawn and quartered for high treason.

Fr. Campion and his associates rejoiced in God, quoting the Scriptures for their own comfort and the edification of others. They were then taken back to prison and chained up to await the queen's pleasure and God's mercy.

The following day, the second batch of priests received the same unjust verdict, apart from John Collington, who was acquitted by the testimony of Mr. Lancaster. Lancaster vouched that he was with Collington in Gray's Inn on the day he was allegedly plotting in Rheims, a place he had never even been to in his life. Fr. Collington was instead banished and lived to be the first Dean of the English Chapter created by the Bishop of Chalcedon.

Innocent of the crimes with which they were charged, the others were to be put to death for their religion.

Edmund Campion spent the time before his execution preparing himself through spiritual exercises. He continued to show great patience and spoke so kindly to his jailer that when the keeper had Norton in his protection afterwards, (a man who had been a violent persecutor of Edmund and his companions), he commented that the difference in behaviour between the two prisoners was like that between a saint and a devil.

In the meantime, the Protestants continued their attempts to get some sort of conformity from the famed Jesuit. The Lieutenant of the Tower even told Edmund's sister, when she visited him three days before his death, that if he changed his religion, he would receive £100 a year for the rest of his life. However, Edmund was well versed in the great lesson 'What will it profit a man to gain the whole world and lose his own soul?'

On the morning of 1st December, he was brought to Coleharbour prison to meet his companions in execution, Ralph Sherwin and Alexander Briant. After embracing, they were led to the awaiting hurdles. Edmund saluted the gathered crowd with the words:

"God save you all! God bless you, and make you all good Catholics!"

They were then drawn to the Tower, Edmund on one hurdle, and the other two sharing another. They were abused and harangued by the crowd all the way, and were called upon to conform by Protestant ministers. Some consulted Edmund on matters of conscience and religion but many spat on him. However, he just courteously wiped his face and remained patient. As he passed Newgate Arch, he lifted himself as best as he could manage to salute the statue of Our Lady that still stood there.

Some members of the Privy Council waited at the place of execution, along with many other persons of note and a vast crowd. Fr. Campion was the first to be brought to the cart beneath the gallows. After a small pause, he began to speak on the text of St. Paul, I Cor. iv. 9, but was interrupted by Sir Francis Knowles and the sheriffs, who urged him to confess his treason against the queen and admit his guilt. Edmund replied: "For the treason which has been laid to my charge and I am come here to suffer for, I desire you all to bear witness with me that thereof I am altogether innocent."

One of the Council suggested that his guilt had already been proved by the law, prompting Edmund to stoically respond:

"Well, my lord, I am a Catholic man and a priest. In that faith have I lived, and in that faith do I intend to die; and if you esteem my religion treason, then am I guilty. As for any other treason, I never committed, God is my judge; but you have now what you desire. I beseech you to have patience, and suffer me to speak a word or two for discharge of my conscience."

However, they would not allow him to go forward and limited the amount of time for which he was permitted to speak. Thus, he protested his innocence of all treason and conspiracy, desiring people to believe the last words he

spoke before his death. He forgave the jury who had been easily deceived and pleaded for the forgiveness of those whose names he had been tricked into giving whilst being tortured (he was told that they would not be touched). Furthermore, he also explained a letter he had sent to a fellow prisoner called Mr. Pound, in which he had said he would not disclose the secrets of some houses where he had been entertained. Although this letter had been misinterpreted by his enemies to mean treason or conspiracy, the secrets he actually meant were where he had said Mass, heard confessions, preached, and performed other priestly duties. He vowed before God that this was the truth.

He was then pressed to declare his opinion of Pius V's Bull excommunicating the queen. When he refused to answer, they questioned whether that meant he renounced the Pope. Answering that he was a Catholic, he was interrupted by the accusation: "In your Catholicism all treason is contained."

With that, Edmund prepared to drink his last draught of Christ's cup. However, his final prayer was interrupted by a minister who wished him to pray with him instead. Turning towards the man, Edmund meekly replied:

"You and I are not one in religion, wherefore I pray you content yourself. I bar none of prayer, only I desire them of the household of faith to pray with me, and in my agony to say one Creed."

Others urged him to pray in English rather than Latin but he answered that he would pray in a language that he understood well. He was then willed to ask for the queen's forgiveness and to pray for her.

"Wherein have I offended her? In this I am innocent. This is my last speech - in this give me credit - I have and do pray for her."

Lord Charles Howard asked him for which queen he prayed and he answered that it was for "Elizabeth, your queen and my queen".

With that, the cart was pulled away and Edmund yielded his soul unto his Saviour, protesting that he died a perfect Catholic. Standing nearby was a youth called Henry Walpole, whose white doublet was stained with the martyr's blood; in time, the incident would lead him to become a Jesuit martyr.

So sincere were Edmund's protestations of innocence, and the trial so obviously a sham, that many printed books afterwards admitted that the Jesuit was blameless.

*Edmund Campion suffered at Tyburn on 1st December, 1581, aged 42, having renounced a brilliant career for the sake of his conscience. Parts of his body were displayed at each of the four city gates as a grave warning to other Catholics who intended to stand firm in their faith.*

# Ralph Sherwin, priest, Tyburn, 1581

Born in Rodsley, near Longford, Derbyshire in 1550, Ralph Sherwin was the protomartyr of the English College in Rome. He was educated at Exeter College, Oxford from 1568, being nominated to one of Sir William Petre's fellowships at the college through his uncle, John Woodward. On 2nd July, 1574, he received an MA and was noted as "an acute philosopher and an excellent Graecian and Hebrician." When he left the university in 1575, he also left the Protestant religion and headed to the seminary at Douai. After some years studying, Ralph was ordained by the Bishop of Cambrai on 23rd March 1577, along with Laurence Johnson, who was later martyred under the name of Richardson. On 2nd August, he was amongst the first batch of students to be sent from Douai to the newly opened English College in Rome, (with Edward Rishton, who was afterwards condemned with him), where he studied in the seminary till 18th April, 1580, when he began his return to England. On the way, the travelling party stopped off at Milan, where Ralph preached before the Archbishop of Milan, St. Charles Borromeo.

Arriving in England, he immediately set to work with great zeal and charity. However, he was apprehended at the house of Mr. Roscarroke in London on 9th November, 1580, only four months after arriving on the mission, and promptly sent to Marshalsea prison. Here he lay for a month, all the time chained up in a great pair of shackles.

ing day. After this last 'assault', Ralph lay for five days in his cell without any food or speaking to anybody. Throughout this time, he felt like he slept before Jesus on the cross. Finally coming fully around, he found that, miraculously, he had no pain in his joints after the wicked torture.

He was a close prisoner for about a year, during which time he received many ministers, even being offered by the Bishops of Canterbury and London the second bishopric of England if he would go to St. Paul's. He resisted their temptations, earning the admiration of many. On Midsummer Day, 1581, he was called before the Lieutenant of the Tower, along with his fellow prisoners. He was asked if he would go to their Common Prayer service but refused, at which the Lieutenant warned him of a new statute that would be used against him unless he complied.

From then on, as he had done before, Ralph spent his imprisonment in continual prayer and meditation. His prayfulness drew great admiration from his keeper, who always referred to him as a man of God, and the most devout priest he had ever seen. He was brought to the bar with Edmund Campion and charged with being a conspirator in the same fictitious plot. After his condemnation, he wrote the following to his friends:

"Your liberality I have received, and disposed thereof to my great contentation; when hereafter, at the pleasure of God, we shall meet in heaven, I trust you shall be rapid,

> "Innocency is my only comfort against all the forged villainy which is fathered on my fellow-priests and me."

In November, the Knight-Marshal sent a message to the keeper of Marshalsea asking if there were any papists in his prison. If there were, then they should send him the articles of their faith that they were willing to defend and he would soon inform them of when any discussions would take place. The proposal was very popular amongst the Catholics, and Ralph, along with two other priests called John Hart and Thomas Bosgrave, offered themselves to the discourse. Drawing up their questions and subscribing their names, they sent their writings to the said Knight-Marshal. However, the Knight-Marshal did not like the questions much so suggested some others that the priests duly accepted. Thus, the priests looked forward to their forum.

However, before the time came, Ralph was taken to the Tower of London and twice tortured. During his first racking, he was asked where Fr. Campion and Fr. Parsons were at that time and who else he knew in England. Moreover, had he, Ralph Sherwin, ever said Mass in Roscarroke's house and had Roscarroke ever given him any money? After his first racking, his torturers lay him out in the snow overnight before again racking him sadistically the follow-

cum fanore. Delay of our death doth somewhat dull me; it was not without cause that our Master Himself said, 'Quod facis fac cito'.

"Truth it is, I hoped ere this, casting off this body of death, to have kissed the precise glorified wounds of my sweet Saviour, sitting in the throne of His Father's own glory. Which desire, as I trust, descending from above, hath so quieted my mind, that, since the judicial sentence proceeded against us, neither the sharpness of the death hath much terrified me, nor the shortness of life much troubled me.

"My sins are great, I confess, but I flee to God's mercy; my negligences are without number, I grant, but I appeal to my Redeemer's clemency: I have no boldness but in His blood; His bitter Passion is my only consolation. It is comfortable that the prophet hath recorded that He hath written us in His hands, Oh! that he would vouchsafe to write Himself in our hearts; how joyful should we then appear before the tribunal-seat of His Father's glory, the dignity whereof, when I think of, my flesh quaketh, not sustaining, by reason of mortal infirmity, the presence of my Creator's majesty.

vale of misery. To Him, therefore, for all His benefits, all times and for ever be all praise and glory.

"Your tender care always had over me, and cost bestowed on me, I trust in heaven shall be rewarded. My prayers you have still had, and that was but duty; other tokens of a grateful mind I could not show by reason of my restrained necessity.

"This very morning, which is the festival of St. Andrew, I was advised by superior authority that tomorrow I was to end the course of this life. God grant that I may do it to the imitation of this noble apostle and servant of God, and that with joy I may say, rising off the hurdle, Salve sancta crux...

"Innocency is my only comfort against all the forged villainy which is fathered on my fellow-priests and me. Well, when by the High Judge, God Himself, this false vizard of treason shall be removed from true Catholic men's faces, then shall it appear who they be that carry a well-meaning, and who an evil, murdering mind. In the main season, God forgive all injustice, and if it be His blessed will to convert our persecutors, that they may become professors of His truth.

"Prayers for my soul procure for me, my loving patron: and so, having great need to prepare myself for God, never quieter in mind, nor less troubled towards God, binding all my iniquities up in His precious wounds, I bid you farewell; yea, and once again, the lovingest uncle that ever kinsman had in this world, farewell.

"God grant us both His grace and blessing until the end, that, living in His fear and dying in His favour, we may enjoy one the other for ever. Salute all my fellow-Catholics. And so, without further troubling of you, my sweetest benefactor, farewell, On St. Andrew's Day 1581.

Your nephew,
Ralph Sherwin, Priest."

"Our Lord perfect us to that end whereunto we were created, that, leaving this world, we may live in Him, and of Him, world without end. It is thought that upon Monday or Tuesday next we shall be passable. God grant us humility, that we, following His footsteps, may obtain the victory."

Ralph's execution was to be carried out roughly two days after the trial. Having verbally dispatched a minister who tried to persuade him from his convictions as he was leaving court, Ralph remained resolute and pointed to the sun, uttering, "Ah, Fr. Campion! I shall be shortly above yonder fellow."

The day before his death, Ralph wrote to his uncle, John Woodward.

"My Dearest Uncle,

"After many conflicts, mixed with spiritual consolations and Christian comforts, it hath pleased God, of His infinite mercy, to call me out of this

Arriving at the place of execution, after sharing a hurdle with Alexander Briant, Ralph saw Edmund Campion

*continues on page 20*

hanged and butchered. The hangman, his hands still covered in the martyr's blood, then grabbed Ralph and, thinking he would scare him, taunted the priest: "Come, Sherwin, take thou also thy wages." Undeterred, Ralph embraced the bewildered hangman and kissed the sticky blood on his hands, a sight that greatly moved the onlookers. Clambering into the cart, the priest closed his eyes and raised his hands to heaven, spending some time in prayer and contemplation.

Finishing his prayers, he asked if the people wanted a speech from. The answer being positive, Ralph spoke with courage in a loud voice. First, he thanked the three persons of the Holy Trinity for the mercies and blessings bestowed upon him, and was about to give an account of his faith when he was interrupted by Sir Francis Knowles. Sir Francis bade him to confess his treason against the Queen; Ralph rejected the charge. Pressed further, he replied:

"I am innocent of any such crime. I have no occasion to tell a lie; it is a case where my soul is at stake."

He persisted to maintain his innocence, adding that although he may be suffering the infamy of dying as a traitor, he had no doubt of his future happiness through Jesus Christ, in whose death, Passion and blood he trusted. He then offered a prayer in which he recognised his imperfection and sinfulness and continued to protest his innocence, claiming that he only went abroad to save his soul - not to plot against the Queen. Sir Francis continued to bait the condemned priest, prompting Ralph to chastise him:

"Tush, tush! You and I shall answer this before another judge, where my innocence shall be known, and you will see that I am guiltless of this."

"We know you are no contriver or doer of this treason, for you are no man of arms; but you are a traitor by consequence," replied Sir Francis.

Ralph boldly responded, "If to be a Catholic only, if to be a perfect Catholic, be to be a traitor, then I am a traitor."

Barred from speaking any further, Ralph forgave all those who had in any way procured his death. He then prayed to his Saviour, Jesus, and refused to comment on Pope Pius' bull despite provocation. Being willed to pray for the queen, he answered that he had and did. Lord Howard questioned if the queen for whom he was praying was Elizabeth, prompting Ralph to smile and comment:

"Yea, for Elizabeth Queen I now at this instant pray my Lord God to make her His servant in this life, and after this life coheir with Jesus Christ."

Some of the crowd became agitated at this, claiming that he sought to make the queen a Catholic, to which Ralph defiantly replied, "God forbid otherwise."

With that, he suffered bravely, his last words being, "Jesu, Jesu, Jesu, be to me a Jesus!"

*Ralph Sherwin suffered on 1st December, 1581, at Tyburn.*

*"Well, when by the High Judge, God Himself, this false vizard of treason shall be removed from true Catholic men's faces, then shall it appear who they be that carry a well-meaning, and who an evil, murdering mind."*

# Alexander Briant SJ, Tyburn, 1581

orn in Somerset in 1556, the slim and handsome Alexander Briant studied for a short period at Hertford Hall, Oxford. Whilst there, he was a pupil of Fr. Robert Parsons, who was probably instrumental in the young Alexander's conversion to Catholicism. However, he soon left the university and the country, heading for the English College of Douai in 1576. It was here and at Rheims that he continued his studies before being ordained (29th March, 1578) and sent on the Mission in late August 1579. Whilst on the Mission, predominantly labouring in his home county, Alexander even managed to reconcile an elderly gentleman who transpired to be the father of Robert Parsons!

Alexander was captured on 28th April, 1581 in his chamber by a pursuivant called Norton. The priest's chamber was ransacked; three pounds and all his belongings were stolen, including items such as a silver chalice that was only in his temporary keeping. He was imprisoned at the Counter Prison, London, in strict isolation, denied food and drink till he was almost starved to death. Eventually, he somehow acquired a penny's worth of stale cheese, a little bread and a pint of strong beer. However, this all caused his thirst to worsen and he resorted to catching the drips of rainwater that leaked into his cell in his hat.

The day after Ascension Day, he was moved to the Tower of London. Sensing that he may be further starved there, he carried a little piece of his hard cheese with him, which his keeper discovered during a search. Two days after his relocation to the Tower, the priest was brought before the Lieutenant (Dr. Hammond) and Norton. The pair interrogated him but Alexander refused to crack, not confessing where he had seen Fr. Parsons, nor how he had been helped, where he had said Mass, or whose confessions he had heard. Irritated at the resolute character on display, the pair began to torture the unfortunate priest, ordering needles to be driven under his nails. Alexander remarkably remained firm, reciting the *Miserere* and asking God to forgive his tormentors. Dr. Hammond was infuriated that they could not break the priest and howled in annoyance, "What a thing is this? If a man were not settled in his religion, this were enough to convert him."

This did not stop the pair ordering that Alexander be racked mercilessly, his body being viciously torn and disjointed, the sadistic Norton, known as the 'master of the rack', boasting that he would make the priest a foot longer. However, he still would not admit where Fr. Parsons was, nor where the print was located and what books he had sold. Instead, still deep in the torture, Alexander suddenly laughed and taunted his persecutors: "Is this the best you can do? You'll have to do much better if you want anything out of me." The onlookers were aghast and one Protestant minister, there in a vain attempt to make Alexander conform, forgot himself and exclaimed, "It's a miracle!"

Thus, Alexander was sent back to his cell for the night. Despite a raging temperature, pain ripping through his whole body, his senses dead and his open wounds slowly scabbing over, he was again tortured the following day. Aware that he could be racked to death this time, Alexander contemplated the Passion of Christ and readied himself for the end. During the torture, Alexander fainted but they revived him by sprinkling water on his face so that he would be fully conscious of all the pain they inflicted.

Realising they could get no information from him, Norton resorted to a different tactic and asked the wretched priest if the queen was the supreme head of the Church of England.

*continues on page 22*

"I am a Catholic, and I believe in this as a Catholic should do."

Norton menacingly replied that Catholics say the Pope is the head of the Church in England.

"And so say I," came Alexander's steadfast reply.

At that, the Lieutenant began to shout abuse at the poor priest, slapping him about the face. The inquisitors then all left him, saying that the priest should be left on the rack, to which he was still manacled, over night. Seeing that even this threat provoked no confession from him, they ordered he be removed from the device of torture and sent to Walesboure. Thrown into a cell, Briant was unable to move his hands, feet or any part of his body after the savage torture he had lived through. Thus, he lay in his clothes for 15 days without any bedding, suffering awful pain and anguish.

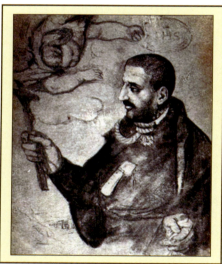

There is no way that the priest could have survived such torments without the help of God as it was all too much for human strength alone. His torments and constancy are comparable to that of the martyrs of the Early Church. Alexander himself admitted that it was only through God that he managed to survive so long. His thoughts were revealed in a letter to the English Jesuits, in which he requested admission into the Society if God spared him:

"The same day that I was first tor-mented on the rack, before I came to the place, giving my mind to prayer, and commending myself and all mine to Our Lord, I was replenished and filled up with a kind of supernatural sweetness of spirit; and even while I was calling upon the name of Jesus, and upon the Blessed Virgin Mary (for I was saying the Rosary), my mind was cheerfully disposed, well comforted, and readily prepared and bent to suffer and endure those torments which even then I most certainly looked for. Whether this that I will say be miraculous or no, God He knoweth; but true it is, and thereof my conscience be a witness before God. And this I say, that in the end of the torture, though my hands and feet were violently stretched and racked, and my adversaries fulfilled their wicked lust in practising their cruel tyranny upon my body, yet, notwithstanding, I was without sense and feeling well-nigh of all grief and pain; and not so only, but as it were comforted, eased, and refreshed of the griefs of the torture bypast. I continued still with perfect and present senses in quietness of heart and tranquility of mind. Which thing when the commissioners did see, they departed, and in going forth of the door they gave orders to rack me again the next day following after the same sort. Now when I heard them say so, it gave me in my mind by-and-by, and I did verily believe and trust that, with the help of God, I should be able to bear and suffer it patiently. In the meantime, as well as I could, I did muse and meditate upon the most bitter Passion of our Saviour, and how full of innumerable pains it was. And whilst I was thus occupied, me thought that my left hand was wounded in the palm, and that I felt the blood run out; but in very deed there was no such thing, nor any other pain than that which seemed to be in my hand."

When the time came for his trial on 16th November, 1581, Alexander made a wooden cross that he carried openly to Westminster Hall. Clutching it during the trial, it was wrested away from, prompting his stinging riposte to the judge, "You can take it out of my hands, but not out of my heart." He had also managed to shave his crown in answer to those ministers who had mocked him for not doing so, alleging that he was ashamed of his vocation. On being condemned, he was immediately restrained with irons, these not being removed till his martyrdom.

He was executed with Edmund Campion and Ralph Sherwin on 1st December, 1581. After these two had been executed before his eyes, Alexander was ordered up into the cart. Having prepared himself to die, Alexander declared that he had been raised as a Catholic and studied at Oxford. Someone interrupted him at this point; "What have we to do with Oxford? Come to thy purpose and confess thy treason."

Calmly, he responded, "I am not guilty of any such thing; I was never at Rome nor at Rheims at that time when Dr. Saunders came into Ireland, the time of the pretended conspiracy."

In this manner he continued to speak, protesting his innocence. However, he did not talk for long but was still pressed to share his thoughts about Pius V's papal bull. He said that he believed it as all Catholics did. Thus, he declared that he died a true Catholic and began to pray.

As he was saying, "*Miserere mei Deus*", the executioner pulled the cart away but through incompetence or malice, Alexander died more painfully than the previous two due to the hangman adjusting the noose, causing extra, unnecessary suffering. After he had been beheaded, dismembered and his heart, bowels and entrails burnt to the glee of the watching crowd, the remains of his body were held up for mocking.

Alexander was only 25 years-old when he suffered and was a learned man, who preached wisely based on his great zeal, patience, constancy and humility.

*Alexander Briant suffered at Tyburn on 1st December, 1581, having had his previously mentioned request to join the Jesuits accepted by the Order.*

# John Payne, priest, Chelmsford, 1582

Little is known of John Payne's early life except that he appears to have been a native of the diocese of Peterborough and a Protestant because he later referred to his brother as a "very earnest Protestant". Thus, it is likely that John too was raised as a Protestant, though the date of his conversion to Roman Catholicism remains unknown. This former Protestantism would explain an incident that happened at Douai College, where he arrived in 1574 and became bursar, the college diarist noting he was "*matures*" and "*gravis*" so evidently older than the average student. However, it is here that we find the first moment of note in John's life. Possibly due to his former Protestantism, John was troubled by doubts over the real presence of Christ in the Eucharist, but these doubts were erased when he witnessed a vision of Christ rising from the chalice at the moment of elevation. This incident became widely known and was depicted on the Bosworth Burse with the lines:

At Gwin's first Mass
John Paine once was
Where dowting of ye cupp
Christ God and Man
Rebukt him then
And made him thus geve upp.

Moreover, so newsworthy was the vision that Gregory Martin, co-founder of the college with William Allen, wrote to Edmund Campion describing John as "a man prudent, serious, mature, religious". Therefore, we are presented with a man viewed as a very 'bright prospect' by Douai and one already of significance – not only was he the bursar of the college, but also a man who had been blessed with a vision.

This 'fame' seems to have spread before him. After being ordained at Cambrai (7th April, 1576) he left for England (24th April), with news reaching the college shortly after that all kinds of threats had been made, especially against the three priests who had travelled together (Henry Shaw, Cuthbert Mayne and John Payne) due to conversions they had reportedly already secured. Moreover, their rosaries, notes and other religious objects had fallen into the hands of the authorities, probably after a 'close shave'. It is of note that John travelled with Cuthbert Mayne, who was to become the first martyr of the Mission, something that may well have been in John's mind during his work.

In those early days of the Mission there was no organisation, so priests ranged over many counties trusting to the hospitality of Catholic houses. Thus, John made Ingatesone Hall in Essex his headquarters, home of Anne, Lady Petre, who was an ardent Catholic and provided refuge for a number of priests.

For disguise, John assumed the guise of Lady Petre's steward and was listed as a servant. As well as acting as her personal chaplain, owing to the scarcity of priests and the loose nature of the organisational structure of the English Mission, he also ministered to Catholics in other localities. Thus, a mention of him can be found in London (January, 1579) in the 'Narrative of Henry Chadderton' – "Arriving in London we hired a lodging in the house of a very pious Catholic woman, who was very often visited by one of the Fathers of the Society of Jesus … In the same house also dwelt Mr. Payne, a priest, afterwards martyr." Thus, John, taking disguise in a gentry house, did not merely reside there, lazily serving the owner, but went out to other areas, serving the needs of the people. After all, John was arrested in far away Haddon, Oxfordshire. Furthermore, he wrote to Douai in July 1576:

"On all sides in daily increasing numbers, a great many are reconciled to the Catholic Church to the amazement of the heretics. And when any of them, as does happen, fall into the hands of the enraged heretics, with such fortitude, courage and constancy do they publicly profess the Catholic faith (especially those that are gentlemen) that the heretics are dumbfounded with astonishment. They now

*continues on page 24*

despair of putting them down with violence."

He goes on to urge that more priests are sent to meet the demand, whilst the Protestant ministers continue to fall into disrepute. At first, this may be considered mere hyperbole, but, on further consideration, it would appear accurate. Only a year later, the Privy Council ordered a return to be made of the number of Catholic recusants in each diocese and a determined attempt was made to apprehend seminary priests. Moreover, Cuthbert Mayne, with whom John had travelled to England, was executed in November of that year in Cornwall. This increase in Government action must have been caused by something and that could, quite possibly, have been the increase in Catholicism of which John wrote. Furthermore, at his execution, he had a great number of supporters, possibly demonstrating a Catholic following, whilst the letter itself was sent with George Godsalf, who John had sent to Douai to be ordained. Therefore, John appears to have gained a significant number of converts.

On 9th February 1577, Douai heard that John had been arrested in Ingatestone and "professed his faith with fortitude" to his captors. However, for some unknown reason, he was released a month later. This is all the more surprising when it is considered that Cuthbert Mayne was executed only nine months later. After that, John appears to have gone back and forth between England and the continent. For example, he was present at Ingatestone Hall in June 1578 to sign Lady Petre's will, but was then recorded as being in Paris in April 1580, according to a government list of resident papists. Moreover, he was at Ingatestone during the Christmas of 1579, because he does not deny George Eliot's claim at his trial "that at Christ's nativity come two years being at my Lady Petre's house, he [Eliot] fell into acquaintance with one Pain a priest, that exercised the office of a steward in the house". Therefore, although little is known of John's activities during this period, it would appear that he was very active.

However, in mid-July 1581, John Payne was arrested with Fr. Godsalf for saying Mass at Haddon in Oxfordshire. He was imprisoned in the Tower of London, where he was viciously racked on several occasions, as well as being treated with disgusting cruelty by all his guards. Occasionally, he was asked whether he would conform, which they said would save his life. Defiantly, the embattled priest intelligently replied, "Why, you say I am in for treason; discharge me of that and then you shall know further of my mind for the other." After one of John's excruciating rackings, the Lieutenant of the Tower sent his servant with a letter reading: "I have herewith sent you pen, ink, and paper, and I pray you write what you have said to Eliot, and to your host in London, concerning the queen and the State; and thereof fail not, at you will answer at your uttermost peril."

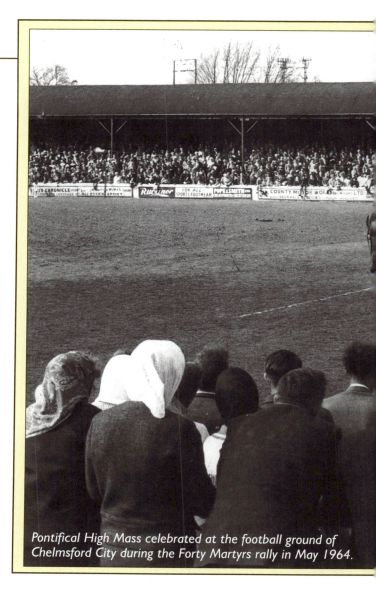

*Pontifical High Mass celebrated at the football ground of Chelmsford City during the Forty Martyrs rally in May 1964.*

John's reply, despite his hands being practically useless after the tortures, was bravely defiant:

"Right Worshipful, my duty remembered, being not able to write without better hands, I have by your appointment used the help of your servant. For answer unto your interrogations, I have already said sufficient for a man that regardeth his own salvation, and that with such advised assertions uttered as amongst Christian men ought to be believed, yet once again briefly for obedience sake.

"First, touching her Majesty, I pray God to preserve her Highness to His honour and her heart's desire; unto whom I always have, and during life will wish, no worse than to my own soul. If her pleasure be not that I shall live and serve her as my sovereign prince, then will I willingly die her faithful servant and, I trust, God's true servant.

"Touching the State, I protest that I am, and ever have been, free from the knowledge of any practice whatsoever, either within or without the realm, intended against the same; for the verity whereof, as I have often before you and the rest of her Grace's commissioners called God to witness, so do I now again; and one day before His Majesty the truth not now credited will be revealed.

chaining him up during the escort. In the meantime, Lady Hopton helped herself to the poor priest's purse.

At his trial, George Eliot gave a statement that "John Payne said Masse at Mr. Willem Moore his house at Haddon upon Sundaye being the second of Julye". George 'Judas' Eliot was the informer, a man who had apostasised and turned to betraying priests to escape persecutions for other offences. He was involved in the arrests of at least 30 priests, including Edmund Campion, and, from what is recorded at John's trial, he appears to have been a known rapist and murderer. Without going into details of the trial, Eliot cast John as one of the prime movers in the 'Rome and Rheims Plot'; there was no proof in these charges contained in the indictments, which accuse them of plotting treason at Rheims. To put it bluntly, Eliot invented the plot, which is even more obvious when it is considered that others who were indicted for involvement in the plot could not possibly have been participants – Edmund Campion was in Prague lecturing, Mr. Bosgrove was not even a seminary priest and the Earl of Arundel was still a Protestant! Furthermore, John continually pledged allegiance to the queen and forgave Eliot for all the wrongs he had caused. Eliot's charges against John were made clear at Edmund Campion's trial:

"Pain … ventured to dissuade him [Eliot] from his allegiance to her majesty, and to become subject to the Pope; affirming that her highness could not live for ever, and that shortly after her days the Catholic religion should be restored. For the furtherance whereof the Catholics beyond the seas had already devised a practice that fifty of them … should come to the court furnished with privy coats, pocket dagger and two-handed swords … and then some of them should set upon her majesty … adding further that if he had place and opportunity convenient he would stab her majesty with a dagger himself, for he thought it no more unlawful to kill her than a brute beast."

John denied all the charges, repelling Eliot's claims – the only evidence brought against him – on several points. Firstly, he swore that as God was his witness, he had never had such a conversation with Eliot. Secondly, he supplied evidence from the law that no man could be condemned without the testimony of two witnesses. Moreover, he proved that Eliot could certainly not be trusted as a reliable witness because he was a notoriously cruel and lewd man, known to have raped a poor woman, as well as stealing from his former mistress, Lady Petre. Furthermore, John underlined that Eliot was of a dubious character because he regularly changed his religion so obviously did not have a reliable conscience, and he was linked to various other crimes, including murder and providing false-witness.

However, the jury still quickly found John guilty of treason. The following day, Saturday 31st March, he was brought before Judge Gaudy for sentencing. The judge

*continues on page 26*

"For Eliot, I forgive his monstrous wickedness, and defy his malicious inventions, wishing that his former behaviour towards others, being well known, as hereafter it will, were not a sufficient disproof of these devised slanders.

"For host or other person living in London or elsewhere (unless they be by subornation of my bloody enemy corrupted), I know they can neither for word, deed, or any disloyalty justly touch me. And so before the seat of God, as also before the sight of men, will I answer at my utmost peril.

"Her Majesty's faithful subject and your worship's humble prisoner, John Payne, priest."

On 20th March, 1582, Sir Owen Hopton, Lieutenant of the Tower, came to John's cell, woke him roughly and ordered him out of the door, the priest only half-dressed. Being told that he was being sent to Chelmsford in Essex for trial, John asked if he could return to his cell to get dressed properly and retrieve his purse. Cruelly, these simple requests were denied and he was brought to trial at Chelmsford according to the Privy Council's decree, wearing only his cassock all the while. Reportedly, John was so sincere and noble that the guards did not even bother asked the priest what he had to say for himself, prompting John to firmly reply that he had already said everything that was necessary and that it was against the law of God and man to condemn a man on the evidence of a notorious felon and liar. Sarcastically, the judge replied that if John was not guilty then the jury would have found him so. Remaining calm despite knowing what surely awaited him, John said that the jury members were not learned men who understood the law but "if it please the queen and her council, I shall die, I refer my cause to God." In response, the aloof judge said that John's own words condemned him and if Eliot had lied, then it was Eliot who caused his death and nobody else. Thus, Judge Gaudy metaphorically washed his hands of all guilt in John's death.

John's final words before sentencing were that treachery was seeking his death but it did not stop the sentence of death being delivered. Demanding to know when he should die, John was told Monday 2nd April at eight o'clock in the morning. He was then returned to prison (believed to be in Colchester Castle, although some argue Chelmsford gaol), where the High Sheriff and others came to visit him, demanding to know whether the priest made Jesus Christ the only cause of his salvation. John calmly told them that this was the case and continued to assert the Catholic truth. The following day, Sunday, till about five o'clock in the afternoon, John was barracked by two men, Dr. Withers and Dr. Sone, who continually tried to make him conform, which they said could save his life.

any treason against the queen. Rather, he had always wished her well, praying that God would grant her a prosperous reign and everlasting life.

Lord Rich, in attendance to oversee the execution, then demanded John confess his treason and express remorse. Patiently, John replied that to admit a falsehood was to condemn his own soul: "I confess truly that I die a Christian Catholic priest. Sweet my Lord [Rich] certify her Majesty thereof, that she suffer not hereafter innocent blood to be cast away, seeing it is no small matter."

Some present claimed that he had confessed his treason to Lady Poole, but John swore that he had never met or knew such a person. Others claimed that John had confided all to his brother several years before, causing John to exclaim: "Bone Deus! My brother is, and always hath been, a very earnest Protestant; yet I know he will not say so falsely of me." Thus, his brother was called for to vouch for John's loyalty, although he did not make it in time. However, his brother, Jerome, as a servant to one of the conspirators, was suspected of complicity in the Babington Plot and spent two years (1586-1588) in the Tower. Moreover, he apparently had Catholic sympathies, for he visited Douai on 22nd October 1581 and under the alias of Millward stayed ten days at the hospice in Rome in 1601. Therefore, it could be conjectured that if Jerome was the mentioned Protestant brother, then he may have been one of John's converts, who appear to have been numerous judging by the crowd at his execution and the letter he had previously written.

> "On all sides in daily increasing numbers, a great many are reconciled to the Catholic Church to the amazement of the heretics."

Late that evening, some Catholics also visited him and John confessed that the two men with whom he had been forced to spend the day had much irritated him with their foolish babblings when he could have instead been preparing himself.

The following morning, 2nd April, 1582, John was tied to a hurdle and drawn to the spot of execution in Chelmsford at the specified time. Being untied from his transport, John knelt and prayed for almost half an hour before rising and walking over to the instrument of his death. Kissing the gallows, he continued to smile and began to mount the ladder. With the noose fitted around his neck, he raised his eyes and hands to heaven for several minutes, then began to address the gathered throng.

First, John made a declaration of his faith, including a full statement of belief in the Holy Trinity. He then desired God to forgive him his sins and have mercy upon all sinners. Next, he forgave all who had wronged him, naming Eliot specifically, who he prayed God would have mercy on. Finally, he declared that his feet had never trodden, his hands had never written and his mind had never thought of

However, the authorities would not wait for his brother to arrive. John continually stated that he died a Catholic priest. Some ministers then demanded that he pray in English with them but John ignored the goading and instead prayed, eventually answering that he had prayed in a tongue he well knew.

With that he was turned off the ladder, but the crowd bayed for him to be hanged before the drawing and quartering was carried out, people pulling his feet down to quicken the agonising, choking death. He had been well-known in the locality, admired by many, and the crowd that witnessed the execution prevented the hangman from cutting his body from the gallows, and disembowelling it, until the priest was completely dead. The crowd only saved such a call for those who were popular or even loved. Therefore, in light of what we have learnt earlier regarding John and conversions, we must consider whether many of this crowd were Catholic, or at least had sympathies with John, hence their shouts. No doubt they were greatly moved by the pious priest crying out, "Jesus, Jesus, Jesus!" whilst he hanged.

# Luke Kirby, priest, Tyburn, 1582

Luke Kirby was born at Bedale in Yorkshire around 1549. After graduating as a Master of Arts from Cambridge, he was reconciled to Catholicism at Louvain and headed to Douai, where he was received into the English College in 1576. He was ordained at Cambrai in September, 1577 and left Rheims for England on 3rd May, 1578. However, he returned to Rheims shortly after on 15th July and from there proceeded to Rome, where he took the oath of the English College on 23rd April, 1579. Unable to contain his zeal for the Catholic faith, Luke sought to convert Protestant visitors to the city, apparently causing one goldsmith there on business to leave the city long before he intended! However, he was unfortunately taken in by a spy called Munday, which led to a lengthy and somewhat sensationalised file on the young priest existing

For being pricked in conscience with our unjust condemnation, which hath happened contrary to his expectation, albeit he offered matter sufficient in his first book of recantation for our adversaries to make a bill of indictment against us, yet he minded, 'expected,' then nothing less, as now he protesteth. He knoweth in conscience our accusations and the evidence brought against us to be false, and to have no colour of truth, but only of malice forged by our enemies; and for Sledd and Munday, he is himself to accuse them of this wicked treachery and falsehood, and of their naughty and abominable life, of which he was made privy, and which for shame I cannot commit to writing. In detestation of his own doings and of their wickedness, he is minded never hereafter to ascend into pulpit, nor to deal again in any matter of religion; for which case he has for-

> "I do acknowledge to my queen as much duty and authority as ever I did to Queen Mary, or as any subject in France, Spain, or Italy doth acknowledge to his king or prince."

back in London even before he left for England.

After spending time in the English College there, Luke headed to England in June, 1580 but was captured the second he stepped off the boat at Dover, and committed to the Gatehouse prison in Westminster. On 5th December, Luke, Thomas Cottam and several other priests were brought to the Tower after being imprisoned elsewhere. On the 10th, Luke and Thomas Cottam suffered the awful torture of the 'Scavenger's Daughter'. The unfortunate priest was encased in a hoop of iron, his whole body folded and bound up in this device like a ball. He was left in this excruciatingly painful position for over an hour.

On 17th November, 1581, Luke was sentenced to death with Edmund Campion and the others accused of the false plot. However, he was not executed until 30th May, 1582 (from 2nd April till the day of his death, he was continuously kept in irons). The following letter was written whilst he awaited his death:

"My most hearty commendations to you and the rest of my dearest friends. If you send anything to me, you must make haste, because we look to suffer death very shortly, as already it is signified to us. Yet I much fear lest our unworthiness of that excellent perfection and crown of martyrdom should procure us a longer life.

"Within these few days John Nichols came to my chamber-window with humble submission to crave mercy and pardon for all his wickedness and treacheries committed against us, and to acknowledge his books, sermons and infamous speeches to our infamy and discredit to be wicked, false, and most execrable before God and man. Which, for preferment, promotion, hope of living, and favour of the nobility, he committed to writing and to the view of the world; whereof being very penitent and sorrowful from his heart, rather than he would commit the like offence again, he wisheth to suffer a thousand deaths.

saken the ministry and is minded to teach a school, as I understand by him, in Norfolk. In proof whereof he showed me his new disguised apparel, as yet covered with his minister's weed. I wished him to make amends for all his sins, and to go to a place of penance; and he answered me, he was not yet conformable to us in every point of religion, nor ever was, but lived at Rome in hypocrisy, as he hath done ever since in his own profession. Again, he thought, that if ever he should depart the realm, he could not escape burning.

"He offered to go to Mr. Lieutenant and to Mr. Secretary Walsingham, and declare how injuriously I and the rest were condemned, that he himself might be free from shedding innocent blood, albeit he was somewhat afraid to show himself in London, where already he had declared our innocent behaviour, and his own malicious dealing toward us in his book and sermons.

"To give my censure and judgment of him, certain I think that he will within a short time fall into infidelity, except God of His goodness in the meantime be merciful unto him, and reclaim him by some good means to the Catholic faith; yet it should seem he hath not lost all good gifts of nature, whereas in conscience he was pricked to open the truth in our defence, and to detect his own wickedness, and treacheries of others practised against us to our confusion. Now I see, as all the world hereafter shall easily perceive, that the doings of this man do confirm the old saying, that rather than God will have wilful murder concealed, He procureth the birds of the air to reveal it.

"I am minded to signify to Sir Francis Walsingham this his submission unto us, except in the meantime I shall learn that he hath (as he promised faithfully to me) already opened the same. Mr. Richardson and Mr. Filby have now

*continues on page 28*

obtained some bedding, who ever since their condemnation have lain upon the boards. Mr. Hart* hath had many and great conflicts with his adversaries. This morning, the 10th of January, he was committed to the dungeon, where he now remaineth. God comfort him; he taketh it very quietly and patiently. The cause was for that he would not yield to Mr. Reynolds of Oxford in any one point, but still remained constant the same man he was before and ever. Mr. Reynolds, albeit he be the best learned of that sort that hath from time to time come hither to preach and confer, yet the more he is tried and dealt withal, the less learning he hath showed. Thus beseeching you to assist us with your good prayers, whereof now especially we stand in need, as we, by God's grace, shall not be unmindful of you. I bid you farewell, this 10th of January 1582. - Yours to death and after death, Luke Kirby."

Luke was correct – John Nichols did confess that he had borne false witness but Sir Owen Hopton suppressed the revelation. Nichols also confessed his crime to Lord Burleigh, one of Queen Elizabeth's principal advisors, but he merely indicated that they had known he was a liar all along.

Having been brought to Tyburn on the day of his execution with Fr. William Filby, Luke was forced to watch his companion's death. After watching this gruesome spectacle, he was lifted up into the cart under the gallows, where he began to speak. The following is a rough record of what was said as his speeches and verbal jousting with others were reported to be very intricate.

"O my friends, O my friends! I am come hither for supposed treason, although indeed it be for my conscience." Luke then started to pray, "O my Saviour Jesus Christ, by whose death and passion I hope to be saved, forgive me, sinful sinner, my manifold sins and offences."

Luke was then manhandled into facing the device of execution where Filby's body was about to be beheaded. The gruesome act completed, the executioner held up the severed head and brandished it towards the condemned priest, shouting "God save the Queen!" In response, Luke simply said "Amen". Hearing this reply, his executioners asked him to which queen he wished God's aid. In response, he replied that it was Elizabeth, to whom he prayed God would send a long and prosperous reign, as well as preservation from her enemies. Seizing this last comment, a minister named Clarke ordered Luke to add "From the Pope's curse and power" on the end of his just-stated wishes. Luke remained calm and outwitted the clumsy minister and his barbs:

"If the Pope levy war against her or curse her unjustly, God preserve her from him also, and so direct her in this life as that she may further and maintain Christ's Catholic religion, and at last inherit the kingdom of heaven."

After this, he made a solemn protestation of his innocence, adding that if any man could bear witness to him being guilty of the charges, then he would throw himself

upon the queen's clemency. Seeing that one of the false witnesses, Munday, was present, Luke requested that the accuser be brought up to relay the evidence. Munday obliged, claiming that whilst he was in Rome, Luke had persuaded him and another young man called Robinson to stay in the city and not return to England as there was shortly to be a rising there. Munday continued by claiming that the priest went further when he saw the pair would not heed his warning, telling them to warn all their Catholic friends about this great day that was nearly upon them. Luke dryly responded without hesitation by telling the crowd and Munday that this was unlikely because he knew that Munday was a Protestant when he had met him.

Munday still maintained his pretence, claiming that it was true and that Luke had even given him some holy pictures to take back to England with him. The condemned priest rejected these falsehoods, claiming that as he never trusted Munday, he certainly would never have given him any pictures. He did say that he gave his accuser two Julios with which to buy pictures and thus he felt very hard done by that this man, who he had helped despite his religion, should now be his accuser. The priest continued by saying that he had regularly helped Protestants, giving them the shirt off his own back or guiding them 40 miles for their safe journey, all out of goodwill despite repeated warnings that this could cause him trouble. As for Munday, Luke said that he had even written to a friend in Rheims, asking him to give the accuser 15 shillings to help him on his way. Obviously, Munday never received this money as he never bothered going that way. Thus, he urged Munday, in the fear and live of God, to tell the truth. Finally, Luke attested that another of his accusers, the Nicholls mentioned in the letter, had even visited him in prison and before four witnesses, including the prison guard, had recanted and admitted that he had made up all of the charges he placed against the unfortunate priest.

Here, the Sheriff interrupted him, "Even as he hath recanted his error and is sorry for it, so do you."

Luke just ignored this interjection and continued to prove that Munday had admitted that all his accusations were fabrications in front of Sir Owen Hopton and some others. Munday rejected this yet Luke still insisted the point but to no avail.

His answers to the six articles were then read. On the first article, he was examined as to his thoughts on Pius V's excommunication of Elizabeth. The priest replied that it was a fact and they would have to speak to the Pope about it. As for the Pope's power to depose princes for certain causes, he replied that it was a point of debate amongst theologians and he could only give his opinion on the matter. Anyway, he concluded with the following:

"I do acknowledge to my queen as much duty and authority as ever I did to Queen Mary, or as any subject in France, Spain, or Italy doth acknowledge to his king or prince. And as for Dr. Saunders and Bristow, they might err in their private opinions, the which I will defend no further than they do agree with the judgment of Christ's Catholic Church."

Pressed as to whether he viewed the queen as head of the Church in England, he replied that he readily yielded to her authority as any subject ought to their monarch but he could go no further because of his conscience. This prompted Sheriff Martin to inform the condemned priest that the queen was merciful and would spare him if he confessed his duty towards her and forsook "that man of Rome". Luke remained steadfast though, answering that to deny the Pope's authority was to deny his faith - it may save his mortal life but it would damn his soul for eternity.

Still his executioners pressed on, telling him that if he admitted his guilt then the queen may spare him. Again, the stoical priest stood firm and said that his conscience knew he had never offended anyone so he would not confess to something he had not done nor ask forgiveness for an act he had not committed. The Sheriff then went even further: "Well then, do but acknowledge those things which your fellow Bosgrave hath done, such as appeareth by his examination, and I will yet save your life." Again, Luke refused, knowing that these farcical offers were evidence that they knew he was innocent but did not want to admit it.

The people then began to shout out, "Away with him", prompting the priest to begin to pray in Latin. The ministers asked him to pray in English so that they could join him but he retorted that by praying with them, he would be dishonouring God. He continued by saying that if they were of the same faith then he would pray with them, before he requested that all the Catholics present join him in prayer.

After he had finished his *Pater Noster* and had just started an *Ave*, the cart was pulled from under him and he was hanged till he was dead. Before he was cut down and his body butchered, two other martyrs of that day, Frs. Thomas Cottam and Laurence Richardson, were forced to take a look at the limp body of the dead priest.

Luke Kirby suffered at Tyburn on 30th May, 1582, effectively delivering his first sermon on the mission whilst standing under the noose that would kill him.

*\*This is Fr. John Hart. After leaving Oxford University, he was ordained at Douai in 1578. Having being captured in June, 1580, he was cruelly tortured and sentenced to death. However, on the day of his execution, he was for some reason granted a reprieve and instead exiled, becoming a Jesuit whilst on the continent. He died in Poland in 1594.*

# Canonisation of the Forty Martyrs

Sunday 25th October, 1970 – the day that St. Peter's basilica in Rome became the parish church of England and Wales. It was on this day that Pope Paul VI canonised 40 of the nearly 400 men and women who gave their lives rather than deny their faith during the turbulent years of the 16th and 17th centuries.

By 7.30am some of the 10,000 pilgrims who had made the journey to Rome were already taking their places but it was not until nine o'clock that the long procession of numerous members of the Church hierarchy began filtering into the basilica. The whole hierarchy of England and Wales (barring Bishop Wheeler of Leeds and Bishop McClean of Middlesbrough who were recovering from illnesses) were situated beside the papal altar, prompting one pilgrim to reportedly wonder aloud, "Who on Earth is saying Mass in England today?" The Pope walked at the end of the procession, dressed in red vestments – the colour of martyrdom.

The canonisation ceremony itself came during the Mass and was started by Cardinal Bertoli, Cardinal Prefect of the Congregation for the Causes of Saints, who spoke in Latin, asking the Pope to perform the act: "That your Holiness inscribes in the catalogue of saints the Forty Blessed Martyrs of England and Wales so that all Christ's faithful may proclaim them as saints."

Fr. James Walsh SJ, vice-postulator of the cause, then read a plea for the canonisation, including short profiles of each of the martyrs, and markedly pointed out that "in our day we are passing through a time of suffering from the human and religious point of view which is in many ways very similar to the experiences of the Forty Martyrs. Today in many parts of the world the followers of Jesus are being put to the severest test for their faith in the gospel and loyalty to the Church. Further, the cold blast of materialism is tending to wither the ideal of life armed and enlightened by revelation and spent in the service of God and man."

The litany of the saints was then sung before the Pope started the solemn proclamation: "to the glory of the holy and undivided Trinity, for the honour of the universal faith and the advancement of Christian life … we decree and define the Forty Blessed Martyrs of England and Wales to be saints."

Pope Paul then recited the 'roll of honour', using the Latinised Christian names for each of the martyrs. Reportedly, he had been diligently practising beforehand with the aid of a tape-recorder. Having heard the final name on the list, the crowd burst into spontaneous applause, which lasted almost a whole minute.

Next, the Pope began his address on the subject of the martyrs, declaring

*continues on page 30*

that the 40 had been "loyal to the Crown" to the end but that "faced with the choice of remaining faithful to the revealed truths of their faith, or of denying them and saving their lives, they chose martyrdom without hesitation." He then went on to quote several of the newly made saints, including Philip Howard and Margaret Clitherow, praising their "freshness and spontaneity", before concluding, "What a need the Church has for such people today."

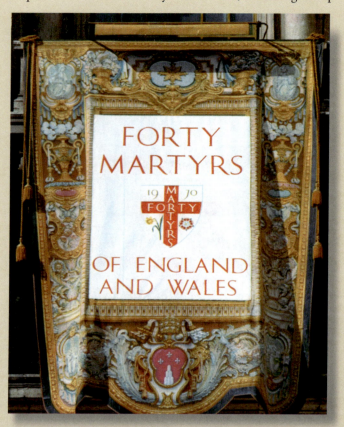

His final prayer, in the wake of welcoming the Archbishop of Canterbury's representative, was that Christians would be united in the same bond of faith and love as the martyrs: "No offence will be inflicted on the honour and sovereignty of a great country such as England. There will be no seeking to lessen the legitimate prestige and the worthy patrimony of piety and usage proper to the Anglican Church when the Catholic Church … is able to embrace her beloved sister in the one authentic communion of the family of Christ. May the blood of the martyrs be able to heal the great wound inflicted upon God's Church by reason of the separation of the Anglican Church from the Catholic Church."

The Gloria from the five-part Mass by William Bird, a famous Catholic of the time who was constantly harassed by the authorities, was then sung before the Mass continued as usual. Notably, at the offertory, the postulators of the cause – the Jesuits Fr. Paul Molinari, Fr. James Walsh, Fr. Philip Caraman and Fr. Clement Tigar – processed with gifts of candles, doves, relics of the martyrs and a huge sheaf of red gladioli, as well as the bread and wine.

The Pope himself gave Communion to several individuals, including 10 year-old Teresa Hynes from Hornchurch. It was her cure from a deadly disease several years before that was reputed to have been a miracle after the intercession of the Forty Martyrs. Communion was also received by 16 year-old Blackburn-resident Keith Matthewman, whose mother's cure from cancer was accepted by Vatican officials as the miracle required for the canonisation of the martyrs.

*Pope Paul VI holds a painting of 'The Transfiguration' by Carel Weight, which he received following the canonisation. With the Pope is Cardinal John Carmel Heenan (centre, wearing glasses and facing camera). (above) The Martyrs' banner hangs in St. Peter's Square.*

# Richard Gwyn, layman, Wrexham, 1584

Richard Gwyn (known as White in English) was born in Llanidloes in Montgomeryshire, Wales, around 1537 and attended university at St. John's, Cambridge, having spent a brief time at Oxford. After completing his studies he became a teacher in Wrexham and then Overton in Flintshire. He and his wife, Catherine, had six children, and Richard steadily acquired a reputation as a Welsh scholar. Throughout, Richard was a church-papist, meaning that he outwardly conformed to Protestantism to the minimum level to keep the authorities off his back whilst he secretly continued as a Catholic. However, his minimal attendance was noted and the Bishop of Chester urged him to conform more regularly. Eventually yielding to this continual pressure, Richard gave in despite his qualms but, as he was leaving the Protestant service, he was attacked by a horde of crows and pecked and battered to the point where he feared for his life. He took this as a providential sign and began to turn towards Catholicism more deeply.

However, with the arrival of the first missionaries from Douai, he stopped the practice of church-papistry at their advice. It was quickly noticed by the authorities that he was no longer attending the Protestant services as the law demanded, so he was arrested and committed to Ruthin jail by Justice Pilson in 1580. He was held there for three months, all the while heavily chained, until the next assizes, when he was brought to the bar. Offered the chance to have his 'crime' forgiven if he would attend just one Protestant service, Richard stood firm and refused the offer, leading him to be returned to prison.

At the assizes held at Wrexham in May of the following year, Judge Bromley was informed of the ongoing situation with Richard and ordered that he should be carried to the Protestant service by force and thus made to attend. Despite putting up a fierce struggle and loudly protesting

*An icon depicting scenes from St. Richard Gwyn's life.*

the violence that he was greeted with, Richard was dragged to the service and laid before the pulpit, still in chains. However, he continued to protest so loudly that neither he nor anyone else could hear the words of the minister, Thomas Jones. Peeved, Judge Bromley ordered him to be taken out and put in the stocks in the market place.

Whilst minister and peasant alike, for a total of ten hours, ridiculed

Richard in the market-square, an indictment was drawn up against him for having "insolently and impiously" interrupted the minister and those attending the service.

A jury quickly found, Richard was brought to the court to answer the charges for himself.

However, as the clerk of the assizes started to read the indictment, Richard suddenly lost his sight.

*continues on page 32*

> *"There is a difference; St. Peter was entrusted with the keys of the Kingdom of Heaven, while the keys entrusted to you are obviously those of the beer cellar."*

Replying to the judge's query of what was the matter with him, Richard replied that he did not know what was wrong with his eyes but he could not see. Sneeringly, the judge replied, "Take care lest the papists make a miracle of this," advising those present not to report what had happened.

Richard was sent back to prison where he was joined shortly after by two other Catholics – John Hughes and Robert Morris. All three were brought to court in 1582 but instead of being charged they were treated to a sermon from a minister of a particularly puritanical outlook. However, the judge's bright plan was given short shrift, the prisoners rapidly responding to the preacher's words by haranguing him in Latin, English and Welsh, leaving the hapless preacher shell-shocked. It is said that during his imprisonment, a minister with a glowing large red nose came to argue about the keys of heaven with Richard, asserting that God had given them to him as well, and not just St. Peter. In response, the prisoner is alleged to have calmly retorted, "There is a difference; St. Peter was entrusted with the keys of the Kingdom of Heaven, while the keys entrusted to you are obviously those of the beer cellar."

After some while, it was announced that all three were to be charged with high treason and they were sent from Wrexham jail to the Council of the Marches in May, 1583, before going on to Bewdley and Bridgenorth. Whilst in the last two places, they were all cruelly tortured in an effort to discover who had reconciled them to the Church. Richard and Hughes courageously held firm but Morris was not so stout, a weakness that he later repented.

Finally, on 9th October, 1584, they were all brought to trial back in Wrexham. False witnesses, notorious for regularly appearing at such trials against Catholics, swore that they had heard them all claim that the queen was not the head of the Church but the Pope, and that the accused had all tried to convert them. The prisoners responded by asserting that these witnesses were infamous for committing perjury. However, their defence was ignored and Judge Bromley ordered the jury to find them guilty, apart from Morris, who, to the surprise of the court, wept that he was not to suffer for the cause like his two companions.

Instead, he was returned to prison. Hughes was subsequently reprieved but Richard suffered according to the sentence at Wrexham on 15th October, 1584. 'Til the last, Richard remained firm, refusing to recognise the queen as the supreme head of the Church despite the offer of his life. Nor would he admit to any treason, answering to the Sheriff's cries that he had committed treason against the queen: "I have never committed any treason against her more than your father or grandfather, unless it be treason to fast and pray [both relatives would, of course, have been Catholics]." Just before he was pushed off the ladder Richard exhorted the crowd to return to the Catholic Church before finishing: "I have been a jesting fellow, and if I have offended any that way, or by my songs, I beseech them for God's sake to forgive me."

Throughout the ordeal, his wife (Catherine) consoled and encouraged him, even when, overcome by emotion, Richard helped the hangman put the noose around his neck. This only heightened his wife's agony, she having already witnessed her husband make the Sign of the Cross on their month-old son's forehead. Furthermore, after her husband had been sentenced to death, Judge Bromley had advised Catherine Gwyn not to follow her husband's evil actions, prompting her to fiercely retort: "If it is blood you want, you may take my life as well as my husband's. Fetch the witnesses and give them a little bribe, and they will give evidence against me too." Despite holding her child in her arms, Catherine spent a couple of days in prison for this perceived insolence.

Richard was cut down from the noose whilst fully alive and butchered in an exceptionally cruel manner. Whilst the hangman's hands were in his bowels, he was heard to say the name of Jesus twice.

His head and one of his quarters were positioned on top of Denbigh Castle, whilst the other three quarters were displayed in Wrexham, Ruthin and Howlet.

Richard Gwyn is the protomartyr of Wales and five of his Welsh-language carols and one funeral ode were discovered and published during the last century.

*The gatehouse of Denbigh Castle.*

# Margaret Clitherow, laywoman, York, 1586

Margaret Clitherow, born around 1553, was the son of the Sheriff of York (1564-5), Thomas Middleton, a candle maker. At the age of 18, she married the butcher and chamberlain of the city, John Clitherow on 8th July, 1571, at St. Martin's on Coney Street. With him, she moved into a house in York Shambles, where she was predominantly left in charge. John was a Protestant but several of his family were recusants and through them,

Margaret began to move in Catholic circles and learn about the faith. Eventually, she converted around 1574, her faith probably bolstered by the return to the city of Fr. John Mush, who it is likely Margaret knew before his ordination. Fr. Mush was Margaret's confessor and would later write her martyrology. From that day, Margaret became a fervent Catholic.

John already had several children but Margaret cared for them as if they were her own. Her husband was fined repeatedly because she would not attend Protestant services, yet he resolutely stood by her. However, Margaret was vocal in her faith and was eventually imprisoned for two years for not attending the parish church. Despite being confined in a filthy, cold, dark hole, fed meagre rations, separated from her loved ones, Margaret still cited the time as "a happy and profitable school" since no one could interrupt her fasting or prayers. During this time, Margaret learnt to read and write, helping to teach Catholic children of the area after her release. Throughout, her husband supported her for she was "a good wife, a tender mother, a kind mistress, loving God above all things and her neighbour as herself."

However, most famous of all was the manner in which she devoted herself and her home to the Catholic cause. Margaret opened her house to harbour priests, including her husband's brother, and it also became a Mass centre. Furthermore, in time, Margaret sent her eldest son to be educated at Douai College on the continent. This last factor led to her being brought in for questioning in 1584, as the authorities desperate to know of her son's whereabouts. Being absent from the country for any serious length of time was interpreted as meaning those involved were Catholics and quite possibly linked to the Mission. Thus, for sending her son abroad, Margaret was confined to her home for a year and a half. However, she continued to make pilgrimages at night to places where Catholic priests had been executed.

John Clitherow remained silent about his wife's activities throughout, possibly demonstrating that he had sympathies with the Catholic cause, but in 1586 he was brought in for further questioning about his son's activities on the continent. Whilst he was thus occupied, the authorities went to search the Clitherow's house and a little Flemish boy guided them straight to some vestments and other articles necessary for the saying of Mass. For this

ST. MARGARET CLITHEROW

*continues on page 34*

punishable with death and left the judge with no choice but to pronounce this sentence; despite his qualms about executing a woman, the Council of the North decreed what he must do. The method of execution for refusing to enter a plea was particularly gruesome and outlined by Judge Clinch: "You shall return to the place from whence you came, and in the lower part of the prison be stripped naked, laid down on your back to the ground, and so much weight laid upon you as you are able to bear, and thus you shall continue three days; the third day you shall have a sharp stone put under your back, and your hands and feet shall be tied to posts that, more weight being laid upon you, you may be pressed to death."

Calmly, Margaret accepted the punishment ("God be thanked, I am not worthy of so good a death as this.") and began to prepare a shift for her martyrdom in the hope that she would be spared the embarrassment of being stripped in front of various onlooking men at her ordeal. During her final imprisonment, Margaret was repeatedly urged to conform to save her life or to at least enter a plea but her self-teaching proving excellent and she ably argued against all the ministers who spoke falsely of Catholicism. Further pressure was put on the young lady when it was discovered that she could be pregnant but still Margaret declined to bow to pressure, refusing to inform the judge that she might be pregnant, which could have saved her life. Instead Margaret declared exactly what was happening to her: "I die not desperately nor procure mine own death; for not being found guilty of such crimes as were laid against me, and yet condemned, I could but rejoice – my cause also being God's quarrel. I die for the love of my Lord Jesus."

Throughout, she continued to show deep love and devotion for her husband and children, often citing her care for them as the reason that she could not enter a plea. Even her stepfather, the mayor of York that year, came to visit her, as well as another clergyman, whom Margaret urged to say no more:

allegedly heinous crime, Margaret was imprisoned in York Castle on 10th March, 1586, and interrogated at length by both civic and ecclesiastical authorities but she would not yield to their urgings for her conformity. Her husband and children were imprisoned at various other places in the city, her daughter Anne being particularly poorly treated, despite being only 12 years-old, for refusing to give information about her mother's activities and continuing to pray in the Catholic manner as she had been taught.

On 14th March, Margaret was charged with treason for having harboured Catholic priests, specifically Fr. John Mush and Fr. Francis Ingleby, and attending Mass. She was arraigned before Judges Clinch and Rhodes, as well as several members of the Council of the North, at the York assizes. However, she refused to enter a plea, saying, "Having made no offence, I need no trial. If you say I have offended, I will be tried by none but by God and your own conscience." Margaret followed this course in the hope of preventing her husband, servants and, particularly, her children from being brought to the trial to give evidence; as a loving mother, she wanted to spare them such an ordeal. Furthermore, they were the only witnesses against her and she did not want them sharing the guilt of her death. Not entering a plea was itself

"I ground my faith upon Jesus Christ, and by Him I steadfastly believe to be saved, as is taught in the Catholic Church through all Christendom, and promised to remain with her unto the world's end, and hell's gates shall not prevail against it: and by God's assistance I mean to live and die in the same faith; for if an angel come from heaven, and preach any other doctrine than we have received, the Apostle biddeth us not to believe him. Therefore, if I should follow your doctrine, I should disobey the Apostle's commandment."

On 25th March, 1586, the dreadful deed was carried out. The night before,

Margaret had endured the dark hours with fear but come the hour, her prayers had left her calm and even joyful. She walked barefoot to the Ousebridge tollbooth, having sent her shoes to her daughter Anne so that she could follow in her mother's footsteps. Still the authorities harangued her, telling her to admit she died for treason despite her protestations of loyalty to the queen: "No, no, Mr. Sheriff, I die for the love of my Lord Jesu." Stripped of even her simple shift, although this was allowed to partly cover her modesty, Margaret's arms were stretched wide apart in the shape of a cross and tied to

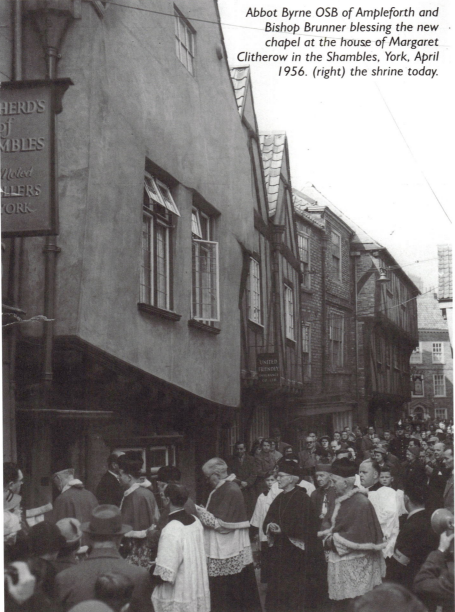

*Abbot Byrne OSB of Ampleforth and Bishop Brunner blessing the new chapel at the house of Margaret Clitherow in the Shambles, York, April 1956. (right) the shrine today.*

poles with cords that she provided. A handkerchief was placed over her face whilst a sharp stone the size of a man's fist was placed directly under her spine in the middle of her back. A door was then placed on top of her and the rocks added by a group of beggars hired for the purpose. As the weight agonisingly built up, Margaret cried out in excruciating pain, "Jesu! Jesu! Jesu! Have mercy on me!" With that, having endured 15 minutes of such suffering, which started at nine o'clock in the morning, her chest gave way and was crushed, her ribs bursting out from under her skin. She was then left in this way for a further six hours to ensure the indignity of her fate.

However, it wasn't the final embarrassment to be heaped upon her. Fr. Mush noted that her remains were buried beside a dunghill in York and were left there for six weeks. Miraculously though, the remains did not begin to putrefy and Catholics eventually collected the incorrupt body parts. Margaret Clitherow's hand is kept in the Monk Bar Convent in York.

Margaret's stepson, William, became a priest, as did her son, Henry, whilst her daughter, Anne, became a nun at St. Ursula's in Louvain.

# Margaret Ward, laywoman, Tyburn, 1588

Margaret Ward was born in Congleton, Cheshire and was in the service of a wealthy London-based Catholic lady by the name of Whittle when Fr. William (or Richard) Watson, author of *Quodibets*, was imprisoned in Bridewell for his religion.

William was a priest from the seminary of Rheims and was a virtuous and zealous missionary. However, after suffering miserably for a while in Bridewell prison, he agreed to attend a Protestant service and was set free immediately after doing so. However, William's torments grew with his freedom, as he began to realise that he had sinned and denied his faith; he felt estranged from God whereas once he had taken great comfort from Him.

Thus, William headed to a nearby prison where some other priests were being held and confessed his sins to them. Receiving absolution, William decided to return to the place of his weakness – the church in Bridewell. There, in the middle of a service, William stood up in front of the whole congregation and announced that he had sinned by attending their service, which was the devil's work rather than God's. He was about to continue but a gang of people assailed him, putting their hands over his mouth and dragging him to prison, where he was thrown in a reeking dungeon which was so awful and cramped that he could not even lie down to go to sleep.

Here they chained him up, feeding him solely on such measly amounts of bread and water that he was lucky to survive. After a month of such wretched treatment, William was moved to a cell above ground where he could at least see some light and had a little more room. However, the adversaries of Catholicism continued to torment him, threatening him and praying in his presence that he would again falter.

Margaret Ward was living in London at the time and, as mentioned above, was in the service of a wealthy lady. Hearing how the priest was being tor-mented, Margaret decided to visit him in an attempt to bring him some comfort. Thus, she headed to the prison with a basket of provisions but was initially refused access to the priest until the jailor's wife intervened for her.

Despite facing many problems, Margaret managed to obtain permission to see William on a regular basis and supply him with necessities upon the conditions that she would be searched when arriving and leaving, and that she could not carry any letters to or from him. For the first month of her visits, these rules were enforced so strictly that the jailors even broke apart the loaves of bread and pies she carried in order to search inside them for any concealed papers. Moreover, at least one jailor was present during their meetings at all times so that their discussions could be heard.

However, after a while, the authorities were convinced that she posed no threat, so they began to be less strict with their searches and not to listen to the conversations. Thus, Margaret had an opportunity to tell William that she had devised a method of escape for him; if he had a piece of rope long enough, he would be able to let himself down from his cell at the top of the prison and escape.

Margaret soon managed to get hold of some rope, which she smuggled into the prison under some food. Furthermore, she found two Catholic watermen who would be waiting with a boat near Bridewell between two and three o'clock the following morning. Disastrously, these two lost their nerve at the last minute, but Margaret was luckily able to find the Irishman John Roche, who was willing to pilot the boat.

When the time came, William secured the rope to the cornice of the building and began to lower himself down. However, by the time he had reached halfway, he realised that the rope was not long enough. Suspended in mid-air, the priest was in severe danger. After pausing, he said a quick prayer and let go of the end of the rope, crashing down with a great noise on top of a shed below.

The fall greatly stunned the unfortunate priest and broke his right arm and leg. However, John Roche immediately ran to his assistance, carrying him to the boat. Coming round as they sailed down the river, William suddenly remembered that he had not removed the rope, placing Margaret Ward in grave danger of retribution if it was discovered by the authorities.

It was too late though; disturbed by the clamour of the priest's fall, the jailor and a number in the neighbourhood had been roused and had already discovered the rope. The jailor was well aware that only one person could have smuggled the rope into the prison so informed the appropriate authorities without delay.

Thus, still in the early morning, a contingent of justices and constables arrived at Margaret's house, just as she was about to leave the lodgings permanently and make good her own escape. Apprehending her swiftly, she was taken to prison and left heavily chained for eight days. During this time, wrote Fr. Robert Southwell to Fr. Acquaviva, S.J.: "She was flogged and hung up by the wrists, the tips of her toes only touching the ground, for so long a time that she was crippled and paralysed, but these sufferings greatly strengthened the glorious martyr for her last struggle."

After eight days of this vicious torture, which included being violently scourged, she was brought, crippled, before the bar. Asked if she was guilty of treason, she responded that if by helping a priest she had committed treason, then she was happy to admit she was guilty and regretted nothing. Despite the judge threatening her and urging her to reveal where the priest was hidden, Margaret would not yield. Thus, they sentenced her to death but said the queen would spare her if she would conform.

However, Margaret replied that she had never offended the queen and believed that the queen would have undertaken exactly the same actions had she known of the pains that the priest was being put through. As for attending a Protestant service, she declined saying that it was against God's Catholic Church so she was happy to lay down her life rather than betray her conscience.

Thus, Margaret Ward was hanged, drawn and quartered at Tyburn on 30th August, 1588, stunning the onlooking crowd by how calm she managed to remain throughout the ordeal.

As for Fr. William, he was recovering in Roche's house and, when sufficiently better, decided that it was time to make his move. Thus, he swapped clothes with John Roche and went on his way. However, John was spotted by the jailor in the priest's clothes and promptly arrested. He was strenuously interrogated and eventually admitted his role in the escape. Charged with treason and subsequently sentenced to death, John echoed Margaret's stance and refused to beg for the queen's mercy or to conform. Thus, he too was executed on the same day as St. Margaret Ward, the pair, along with four other Catholics (Richard Martin, Edward Shelley, Richard Leigh and Richard Flowers), defiantly singing as they went to their deaths. All the martyrs that day were forbidden from speaking to the crowd before being executed because the authorities feared the influence their words might have on the people.

# Edmund Gennings, priest, London, 1591

In 1567, Edmund Gennings (who used the name Ironmonger for disguise whilst on the Mission) was born a Protestant in Lichfield, Staffordshire. He was a very serious child, his brother noting that he did not enjoy the usual children's games "but greatly loved to behold the heavens; and therefore he usually went forth in the evening to delight himself with the sight of the skies bedecked with stars."

His brother continues by saying that it was on one of these nights that the young Edmund saw a vision in the sky. He saw armed men killing and murdering defenceless victims, blood running freely throughout the scene. Fearing what he had seen, Edmund ran home to tell his mother, then a widow. His mother and four neighbours went to the place Edmund told them about and saw the same spectacle. Edmund's brother notes that "This happened at the beginning of our chiefest persecution, not long before the glorious death of Father Campion and the rest."

When he was about 16, Edmund's schoolmaster recommended him to employment as page to Richard Sherwood, a Catholic gentleman. Under Sherwood, a man much persecuted for his faith, Edmund learnt about Catholicism. A year later, Sherwood crossed to Rheims and became a priest in 1584, before being sent on the Mission with Robert Dibdale on 2nd August of that year. Subsequently, Edmund found himself receiving a similar call, and after repeated requests and recommendations to Dr. William Allen (president of the college and later a Cardinal), he crossed to Rheims.

Edmund studied with great diligence, particularly the lives of the saints. He also paid great attention to the fear and love of God, drawing much praise from his superiors. One of them wrote the following: "Edmund Gennings was provident and wise in counsel, humble in obedience, devout in Christ, strong in faith, prompt in good works, most true and sincere in his words, remarkable in his goodness, excellent in charity. He was often afflicted and sick; he suffered all patiently; there was ever in him a discretion in all his actions, and a love towards all worthy of imitation."

Already being of poor constitution, the pains he took in his studies and spiritual exercises further weakened him, to the point that he became gravely ill. This left him with a continual ague and other infirmities, which soon led to consumption. The doctors feared for his life, so Dr. Allen decided to send him to England, hoping that the change of air may cause a recovery.

Reluctantly, Edmund left Rheims but only got as far as Havre de Grace in Normandy. Staying with several exiled English priests, they soon managed to secure him a passage to London within a fortnight, and began to make ready for his departure. However, Edmund, who was reluctant to risk himself amongst his Protestant relations before he had finished his training, was suddenly and miraculously cured after praying at length for his recovery. The other priests still urged him to go but it soon became clear that Edmund was as well as he had ever been in his life. Thus, they relented and were amazed the next day to see him not only hungrily devour some meat, but also to go on a long walk.

His recovery seen as miraculous, Edmund returned to Rheims with renewed vigour. He yearned to return to England and redeem the souls of his neighbours before receiving the crown of martyrdom. It was well known that his favourite expression when talking of martyrdom in England was "*Vivamus in spe, vivamus in spe*", meaning "Let us live in hope, let us live in hope!"

Having seen this fervour, Edmund's superiors at the college procured a dispensation from Rome allowing the young man to be ordained at the tender age of only 23. Edmund prepared himself for this great honour with such devotion and concentration that it caused a gentle shaking in his body that continued until the day he died. Moreover, at this time, owing to his renowned humility, patience and charity, he was made prefect of the hospital. Displaying such diligence in helping the sick, regardless of how unpleasant the task, many viewed him as a perfect example of piety and humility.

He was ordained at Soissons on 18th March, 1590, with Alexander Rawlins, who would later suffer at York in 1595. On 9th April, Edmund was sent on the Mission with the said Rawlins, and another priest called Hugo Sewel. Making their way to the coast, they were attacked by a group of Huguenots from the garrison of Crippy. Robbed of their belongings and stripped of their clothes, the priests were imprisoned by the governor of the town. Threatened with death, they were appallingly treated and thrown into a dark, dank dungeon, where they remained from Tuesday until Thursday night. On 17th April, after their ordeal, Edmund wrote to Dr. Barret (then head of the College at Rheims) informing him that: "we despised their threats, rejoicing that we suffered these cruelties from them, for the self-same causes that we shall suffer death in England, if God gives us strength, so that neither the prison nor the want of meat, clothes, or beds any ways terrified us. On Thursday in the evening, after we had eaten nothing that day but a little black bread, we had our papers restored to us, and we were put out of the town, and about ten o'clock at night we arrived at the suburbs of La Fere, God Almighty showing us the way, which we knew not. When we had here rested our weary bodies, the next day the governor of La Fere gave us a crown, and sent us away in peace, and now we are at Abbeville."

On the very morning of his departure, Edmund prayed that the failure to find his brother would increase his patience, trusting that God's will would be done. His devotions finished, he again set off to say Mass. Returning from the celebration towards his inn, he again felt the same emotions that had struck him before. This time he was on Ludgate Hill. Once more, he fearfully checked behind him. Again, nobody but a youth in a brown cloak. Suddenly it struck him; it was the same man as before. Viewing the figure carefully, for he had not seen his brother for eight or nine years, he realised that this was him.

Approaching the youth, he inquired as to his birthplace. Hearing that the mysterious figure was a Staffordshire man, he asked his name. The answer came back that it was Gennings and the priest knew that he had found his brother. Telling his brother that he was a relative called Ironmonger, he asked what had happened to his brother Edmund. The youth, not knowing that it was to Edmund

> "If to return into England priest, or to say Mass, be Popish treason,
> I here confess I am a traitor; but I think not so, and therefore I acknowledge
> myself guilty of these things, not with repentance or sorrow of heart, but with an
> open protestation of inward joy that I have done so good deeds."

Reaching Treport on the Normandy coast, Edmund and his companions embarked upon a French vessel whose captain promised to set them off in England during the night. They landed near Whitby, in Yorkshire, risking their lives by having to scale a high cliff. Arriving in the town, they went into an inn to refresh themselves. Unfortunately, they were suspected by a man called Ratcliffe, who started to question them about their sudden arrival in the town. However, their time had not yet come, and they satisfied the suspicious mind before making to a Catholic gentleman's house two or three miles outside the town.

The companions then parted. Edmund stayed in the North for six months before returning to his native Lichfield, where he hoped to convert his relatives to the true faith. However, on his return, he discovered that they were all dead apart from one brother, who was apparently somewhere in London. Learning that his brother was something of a pleasure-seeking rogue, he resolved to go and find him, to rescue this strayed sheep. Edmund searched the capital for a whole month but could find no sign of his brother. Thus, he decided to give up the chase for a while.

Leaving the inn in which he was staying for his final days in London, Edmund was passing St. Paul's. Suddenly, feeling his whole body break out in sweat and his hair stand on end, he glanced behind him, fearing what evil was about to befall him. However, all he saw was a youth huddled in a brown cloak. Thinking nothing of it, he made his way to the house in which he was to say Mass that day.

he spoke, informed the stranger that he was gone to Rome and the Pope, and had become a notable papist and traitor both to God and country, who would be hanged if he ever returned. Edmund replied that he had heard Edmund was a good, honest man, who loved his country, but loved God even more.

Edmund chided John (his brother) as to whether he would recognise his brother if he ever saw him. Replying that he would not, John began to become suspicious and added that he feared his brother may be a priest, and would thus place him and his friends in danger. He would respect him but never follow him.

With that, Edmund revealed his true identity but not that he was a priest. John was in no mood for converting though and it was not the time or place to attempt such a thing. Taking his leave of him, Edmund promised to return after his travels, when they would discuss matters of great seriousness. However, the conversion of his brother was only to come about through his own martyrdom.

On 7th November, 1591, Edmund returned to London. At a Catholic house in Holborn, he met a virtuous priest, Polydore Plasden, a fellow student from Rheims. They agreed to say Mass together the following day at the house of Swithin Wells, as it was the Octave of All Saints. The following day, Edmund, Fr. Plasden and another priest named White, were saying Mass for Brian Lacy, John Mason, Sydney Hodgson, Mrs. Wells and some others. As Edmund reached the consecration, Topcliffe, the notorious priest-

*continues on page 40*

catcher, with an assortment of guards, suddenly broke open the door of the room in which Mass was being said. The previously mentioned gentlemen rose from their prayers, seeking to repel the invaders and prevent the profaning of the Blessed Sacrament. One of the laymen (John Mason) charged at Topcliffe, tumbling back down the stairs with him.

Fr. Plasden ordered the others to hold the door against the attackers and urged Edmund to finish the Mass amidst all the confusion. Returning to the door, Fr. Plasden saw Topcliffe storming up the stairs, his head bleeding and threatening to raise the whole street. Fr. Plasden managed to pacify the invading force with the promise that they could take them all peacefully if they just allowed the Mass to be completed. Edmund quickly finished and Topcliffe immediately rushed in, seizing the said priest in his vestments, along with ten others and all the religious apparatus. They were all taken to Newgate prison where they waited for their trials after questioning by Justice Yonge.

Swithin Wells had been absent during the Mass and was shocked to return home and find his house ransacked. Learning that his wife had been imprisoned, he went and pleaded her case to Justice Yonge, as well as demanding the return of his house keys. However, the justice did not hesitate in sending him to join the others, a pair of iron bolts on his legs. Questioning him the next say, Wells said that he had not been privy to the Mass being said in his house but wished he had been, as it was a great honour. Sarcastically, the justice informed him that he may not have been at the feast but he would still taste the sauce.

Edmund and the rest were brought to trial on 4th December. The jury was urged to find them guilty despite the only proof being that one of them had said Mass in Wells' house and that the others had been present. The judges were spiteful and abusive to the defendants, particularly Edmund because of his young age and argumentative responses. Hoping to urge the people into abusing him, the authorities made him wear not the vestments in which they had paraded him triumphantly through the streets, but a jester's coat, which they had found in Wells' house.

The following day, the jury pronounced that the three priests were guilty of high treason for returning into the kingdom. All the rest were guilty of felony for aiding and assisting the priests. They were to die at Tyburn, except Edmund and Swithun Wells, who were to be executed outside Wells' front door in Gray's Inn Fields. After pronouncing sentence, the judges attempted to persuade them to conform to the Protestant faith, promising that they would be pardoned if they did. The response from all was that they would live and die in the true Roman Catholic faith, which they, and all before, had loyally professed. They would not attend a Reformed service nor recognise that the queen was the spiritual head of the Church.

The three priests were cast into the dungeon at Newgate. Justice Yonge, Topcliffe, and a few others visited Edmund on several occasions, promising him his life and liberty if he should go to their church and renounce his own religion. Despite their offers of power and wealth if he conformed, Edmund stood firm. Greatly offended, the visitors had him cast into a dark hole of the prison, where he could not even see his hands in front of his face. It was not even high enough for him to stand in. Without any food or water, the unfortunate priest remained in prayer in that foul place until the hour of his death.

At eight o'clock on the morning of 10th December, Frs. Plasden and White were carried to Tyburn and executed. Mrs. Wells was greatly distressed to be reprieved, and instead died in prison. Edmund and Wells were taken to the door of Wells' house. After preaching from several ministers, Edmund was taken off his hurdle, and, like St. Andrew, joyfully saluted the gibbet prepared for him. Mounting the ladder, the gathered crowd began to ask him questions to which he answered directly.

At length, Topcliffe demanded in a loud voice, "Gennings, Gennings, confess thy fault, thy Popish treason, and the queen by submission no doubt will grant thee pardon."

Edmund responded mildly: "I know not, Mr. Topcliffe, in what I have offended my dear anointed princess; for if I have offended her, or any other, in anything, I would willingly ask her and all the world forgiveness. If she be offended with me without a cause, for professing my faith and religion, because I am a priest, or because I will not turn minister against my conscience, I shall be, I trust, excused and innocent before God. 'I must obey God,' saith St. Peter, 'rather than men'; and I must not in this case acknowledge a fault where there is none. If to return into England priest, or to say Mass, be Popish treason, I here confess I am a traitor; but I think not so, and therefore I acknowledge myself guilty of these things, not with repentance or sorrow of heart, but with an open protestation of inward joy that I have done so good deeds; which, if they were to do again, I would, by the permission and assistance of God, accomplish the same, although with the hazard of a thousand lives."

Infuriated by these words, Topcliffe did not even give Edmund time to pray, ordering the hangman to kick the ladder away. Almost immediately, Topcliffe had the rope cut. Edmund, barely stunned, dropped to his feet and raised his eyes to heaven. Promptly, the hangman tripped him up, causing him to fall on the block where he was to be quartered.

Fully aware during his dismembering, the pain seared through his body and he uttered the words, "Oh, it smarts!" Hearing this, Swithun Wells responded, "Alas! sweet soul, thy pain is great indeed, but almost past; pray for me now, most holy saint that mine may come."

*continues on page 42*

With his body ripped apart and his bowels cast into the fire, the crowd were aghast to hear Edmund utter his last words: "*Sancte Gregori ora pro me*". The executioner, holding Edmund's heart aloft in his clenched hand, looked down aghast and swore loudly, before announcing, "See, his heart is in my hand, and yet Gregory is in his mouth. O egregious Papist!"

A devout virgin, who had dedicated herself to the service of God, was amongst the many Catholics present at the execution. If possible, she wanted to get some part of Edmund's body or blood to keep as a relic. However, she was not able to get near the gibbet, as the crowd was too great. Thus, she followed his quarters as they were carried back to Newgate to be boiled, along with the many others hoping to see the body parts. To satisfy the throng's curiosity, Bull, the hangman, picked up one of the quarters by the arm and held it aloft for the people to see. He then carelessly tossed the body part back into the basket, the arm dangling over the edge. The virgin edged forward, reaching out to touch the hand. For some reason, she decided to give the thumb a tug and it instantly came away in her hand. Quickly, she scurried away so that nobody would notice her.

However, the most wonderful event that followed Edmund's death was the conversion of his brother, John. Initially, John had rejoiced at news of his brother's death, hoping to be safe from any persecutions his brother's religion may have brought upon him. After all, he had been raised to hate Catholicism and was rather inclined towards the puritanical brand of Protestantism. However, about ten days after the execution, having spent all day in frivolous pursuits, he went home, weary of the day's play. At home, his heart began to grow heavy and he began to think on how he had wasted the day. Mingled with these thoughts were visions of his brother's death, and the realisation that not long before, his brother had forsaken all worldly pleasures for his religion. Furthermore, he had been willing to suffer intolerably for it. Considering his own religion and then his brother's Catholicism, he began to see one embracing pain and mortification in comparison to pleasure; one to live strictly, the other licentiously; one to fear sin, the other to enjoy it. John began to weep, realising the error of his ways and prayed for God to help him see the truth. Lying prostrate on the ground, he vowed to forsake kin and country to discover more about his brother's religion. Without telling anyone, he left for Douai College soon after, where he was made priest in 1607, and sent upon the mission in 1608. After a period, he became a Franciscan, procuring a convent for his Order at Douai in 1617. Furthermore, he restored the English Franciscan province, and was its first Provincial. Many of the details of Edmund Gennings' life are only known because of a biography later written by John and published in St-Omer in 1614.

# Swithun Wells, layman, London, 1591

The sixth son of Thomas Wells of Brambridge, Hampshire, Swithun Wells was born in about 1536, and was well educated and very intelligent. A humorous and good-natured character, he was a great lover of hunting, hawking and other such activities but as he grew older, he became more concerned about his faith, establishing a school at Monkton Farleigh, Wiltshire from 1576-1582, through which many Catholic children passed, supposedly including one later-martyr. He conformed outwardly though until the Privy Council ordered a search of his properties on 25th May, 1582, prompting him to be 'fully' reconciled in 1583. In 1585, he moved to London to devote himself to hosting and guiding priests. The house quickly became a Mass centre and Swithun promptly became the subject of many investigations and prison terms, including an examination over his alleged complicity in the Babington Plot in August, 1586.

As we have seen, Swithun was arrested with Edmund Gennings and followed his fate. A letter he wrote to his Catholic brother-in-law, Gerard Morin, whilst in prison before his condemnation, underlines the strength of his faith:

"The comforts which captivity bringeth are so manifold, that I have rather cause to thank God highly for His fatherly correction than to complain of any worldly misery whatsoever. *Dominus de coelo in terram aspexit ut audiret gemitus compeditorum, etc. Potius mihi habetur affligi pro Christo, quam honorari a Christo.* These, and the like, cannot but comfort a good Christian, and cause him to esteem his captivity to be a principal freedom, his prison a heavenly harbour, and his irons an ornament. These will plead for him, and the prison will protect him. God send me withal the prayers of all good folks to obtain some end of all miseries, such as to His holy will and pleasure shall be most agreeable. I have been long time in durance, and endured much pain; but the many future rewards in the heavenly payment make all pains seem to me a pleasure; and truly custom hath caused that it is now no grief to be debarred from company, desiring nothing more than solitariness; but rather I rejoice that thereby I have the better occasion, with prayer, to prepare myself to that happy end for which I was created and placed here by God, assuring myself always of this one thing, that how few soever I see, yet am I not alone. *Solus non est cui Christus comes est* – He is not alone who has Christ in his company. When I pray, I talk with God; when I read, He talketh to me; so that I am never alone. He is my chiefest companion and only comfort. *Cum ipso sum in tribulatione.*

"I have no cause to complain of the hardness of prison considering the effects thereof, and the rather because I fasten not my affections upon worldly vanities, whereof I have had my fill, to my great grief and sorrow.

"I renounced the world before ever I tasted of imprisonment, even in my baptism, which being so, how little doth it import in what place I be in the world, since, by promise, I vowed once never to be of the world; which promise and profession, so slenderly soever I have kept heretofore, I purpose, for the time to come, God assisting me with His grace in my commenced enterprise, to continue to my life's end. The world is crucified to me, and I to the world. God forbid that I should glory in anything but in the cross of Christ. I utterly refuse all commodities, pleasures, pastimes, and delights, saving only the sweet service of God, in whom is the perfection of all true pleasure. *Vanitas vanitatum, et omnia vanitas prater amare Deum* – Vanity of vanities, and all is vanity beside loving God. I am bound and charged with [unknown], yet I am loose and unbound towards God; and far better I

account it to have the body bound than the soul to be in bondage. I am threatened hard with danger of death; but if it be no worse, I will not wish it to be better. God send me His grace, and then I weigh not what flesh and blood can do unto me. I have answered to many curious and dangerous questions, but I trust with good advisement, not offending my conscience. What will become of it, God knows best, to whose perfection I commit you.

'*E carcere et catenis ad regnum,
Tuus dum vixero.*"

Swithun received his death sentence with courage and prepared himself for the event with steady prayer. On the morning of his execution, he was brought out with his wife (also sentenced to death for harbouring priests) and Fr. Gennings, but his wife was sent back to prison almost immediately. She was subsequently imprisoned in Newgate till her death in 1602, during which time she

prayed and fasted regularly.

Swithun was carried with Fr. Gennings to Gray's Inn Fields, where he was to be executed in front of his own house. On the way, he saw an old friend, greeting him jovially: "Farewell, dear friend! Farewell all hawking, hunting and old pastimes; I am now going a better way."

At the place of execution, he first witnessed the bloody butchering of Fr. Gennings. Showing no fear, he remarkably urged the authorities to hasten his death, chiding the notorious pursuivant Topcliffe: "Dispatch, Mr. Topcliffe, dispatch. Are you not ashamed to suffer an old man to stand here so long in his shirt in the cold? I pray God make you of a Saul a Paul, of a persecutor a Catholic professor. I heartily forgive you."

With such brave words, the white-haired Swithun was executed in front of his own front door on 10th December, 1591.

# Polydore Plasden, priest, Tyburn, 1591

Born in 1563 and the son of a London horner, Polydore Plasden operated under the alias Oliver Palmer during the Mission, as well as under the name of Blaxton. His studies were divided between the College of Douai at Rheims and the English College in Rome, where he was ordained on 7th December, 1586. He remained in Rome for a year before staying in Rheims from 8th April to 2nd September, 1588. From there, he embarked upon the English Mission but little is known of his work.

Details of his arrest, trial and condemnation are given in the account of Edmund Gennings' life. Polydore was sentenced to death for high treason - he was a priest who had returned to England to exercise his priestly functions.

He was drawn to Tyburn with Eustace White and hanged, disembowelled and quartered on 10th December, 1591. At his execution, he acknowledged Elizabeth as his lawful queen and said that he would defend her against all her enemies. Moreover, he prayed for her and the whole realm. The people in the crowd were stunned by the sincerity of his words, including Sir Walter Raleigh. Assured that the priest was speaking the truth, the crowd and Sir

Walter began to question why the priest should die but the notorious Topcliffe was not about to let a priest live. Still smarting from the already dead Brian Lacy's taunt ("You yourself in Queen Mary's days were a papist. Tell me, were you also then a traitor?") he knew how to satisfy the crowd's troubles, questioning Polydore, "Would you defend the queen against the Pope if he came to establish thy religion?" Polydore did not waver, declaring, "I would never fight against my religion." Thus, Polydore Plasden's fate was irredeemably sealed but, by the orders of Sir Walter Raleigh, he was allowed to hang till he was dead before the mutilation began.

Three laymen were executed with the priests. Brian Lacy, John Mason and Sydney Hodgson were arrested at the same time as Polydore Plasden and Edmund Gennings. Despite being offered the chance to save their lives through occasional conformity, they elected to stay constant to the Faith and so died for it, charged with aiding and assisting priests.

"I would never fight against my religion."

# Eustace White, priest, Tyburn, 1591

**B**orn at Louth, Lincolnshire in 1560, Eustace White was the youngest of the ten children of the civic head of the area, the earnest Protestant, William White, who was so offended by his son's conversion that he even laid a curse on him! Nevertheless, Eustace travelled to the continent and first entered the College of Douai (1584), then residing at Rheims, before going on to the English College in Rome (1586), where he was ordained two years later. He returned to Rheims in October, 1588, before heading to England on the Mission in November. During his time on the mission, Eustace laboured in the southwest of England.

There is some debate as to where Eustace was arrested. Edmund Gennings' brother, John, who wrote a book about his martyred sibling, claimed that the priest was arrested at the same time as Edmund, at the house of Swithun Wells (A priest called White was arrested at this time but it does not appear to have been Eustace). However, some evidence exists that he had been captured twice before and a letter from Fr. Stephen Barnes to Fr. Barber of Douai gives a different story of Eustace's apprehension that would appear to be more accurate.

Fr. Barnes claimed that Eustace was arrested at Blandford in Dorset. Coming from London, Eustace fell into the acquaintance of a lawyer from the West country. Riding with the lawyer, the priest began to speak about happenings on the continent as if he had merely been there as a traveller. Finding the lawyer favourable to this discourse, the priest began to speak more openly of his religion. Reaching Blandford, Eustace made to go, leaving his travelling companion there. However, the lawyer urged him to stay the night so that they could breakfast together the following morning before taking leave of each other.

Having stayed the night and had his breakfast, the priest bade farewell to the lawyer. Immediately, the lawyer went and informed the local officers that he knew a seminary priest and pointed them in the direction Eustace had headed. Meanwhile, Eustace had realised that he had left his breviary in his room from the previous night so turned back towards the inn to collect it.

It was here that he was captured on 1st September, 1591. He admitted that he was a priest so as not to cause harm to anyone else. Without delay, the captors sent for a learned minister called Dr. Howell to confer with Eustace about his religion. Eustace took for his defence a piece of the scriptures, but the minister insisted that the Bible contained no such words. This argument continued until the Catholic priest promised that he would attend the minister's service if he should be proved wrong. In response, the minister said that he would bring his Bible the following day and if he was wrong, then he would never attend the Protestant service again and become a Catholic.

The next day, the minister returned. Having heard of the argument, a great throng had arrived to see the resolution of the dispute, confident that they would witness the priest being humbled and forced to conform. Arriving in the room, the minister put his bible on the table, leant on it and began to talk about other things. However, Eustace repeated the conditions agreed the day before and asked whether the minister had brought his bible with him. The minister answered positively but still kept his elbow firmly in position and looked to change the subject. Eustace remained firm, declaring that there was no need for any other argument; it would soon be ended with either him a conformer or the minister a Catholic. Still the minister would not budge and Eustace attempted to ease the book from under its pin. The minister still refused to budge so Eustace turned to the crowd, relayed the conditions again and then willed them to judge who was right and who espoused false doctrine. The onlookers were greatly moved and many fervent Protestants were calmed in their zeal for the new religion. A number of Blandford residents even planned to start a petition requesting that the queen spare the priest.

Eustace was detained for several more days before being sent to Bridewell prison in London by a pursuivant on 18th September. Initially, he was kept locked up for 46 days, having only straw to lie on whilst remaining closely manacled throughout the period However, on 25th October, the Privy Council gave the order to examine him under torture. The unfortunate Eustace was mercilessly racked seven times and left at the will of the notorious Topcliffe. He was tortured by other methods too, such as being hung by iron manacles around his wrists for eight hours in an effort to discover where he had said Mass and who had helped him. However, despite sweating profusely due to the agonies he suffered, and being deprived of clothing and food, the priest compromised nobody. During the greatest of the pains he suffered, he was heard to cry out, "Lord, more pain, if Thou pleasest, and more patience." Despite his inhuman treatment, he spoke with humility to Topcliffe:

"I am not angry with you for all this, but shall pray to God for your welfare and salvation."

Enraged, Topcliffe replied that he did not want the prayers of a traitor and would have him hanged at the next sessions.

"Then," spoke Eustace, "I will pray for you, sir, at last, at the foot of the gallows; for you have great need of prayers."

Eustace was tried and sentenced to death with Edmund Gennings, Polydore Plasden and the others on 6th December, 1591. He stood in the same tattered clothes in which he had endured prison, looking wraith-like due to lack of food and the extremities of pain that had been inflicted upon him.

His last words to the gathered crowd baying for blood before his final agony began were: "If I had never so many lives, I would think them very few to bestow upon your Tyburns to defend my religion. I wish I had a great many more than one, you should have them all one after another."

Cut down whilst still fully alive, he rose to his feet only to be tripped up by the executioner and dragged towards the fire. Two men spread his arms and stood on them whilst the executioner butchered him, tearing his tortured body apart, Eustace conscious and aware throughout the whole terrible ordeal.

*Thus, Eustace White was condemned for being a priest and suffered at Tyburn on 10th December, 1591.*

*The capture of St. Edmund Gennings, who was tried and condemned to death with St. Eustace White.*

# John Boste, priest, Durham, 1594

John Boste was born to a gentleman's family in Dufton, Westmorland in about 1544. He attended Queen's College, Oxford University at the same time as Toby Matthews (1569-72), who was Bishop of Durham at the time of John's death and later became Archbishop of York. On hearing that John had been executed, Bishop Matthews was heard to comment "It was a pity so much worth should have died that day."

Having been made a Fellow of the College, John was reconciled to the Church at Brome, Suffolk in 1576. He resigned his fellowship four years later and left the country for the sake of his conscience. He entered the College of Douai at Rheims, was ordained on 4th March, 1581 and then sent upon the English Mission in April, only a month after his ordination, underlining his zeal for the cause.

He landed at Hartlepool and laboured in England with great energy for several years, converting huge numbers of people. Whenever it was possible, John said Mass daily and distributed numerous copies of the Douai New Testament which he had smuggled into the country. He was also known to travel around the area in disguise, dressed as a servant in the livery costume of Lord Montacute. Moreover, he showed no fear whatsoever. Only a few days after arriving in England, he stayed at a parson's house near Norwich! Even more surprising was that he intended to say Mass there whilst the unsuspecting parson was absent but this unbelievable plan was thwarted by the parson's sudden return. Mainly working in the North with the help of the layman John Speed, John would cross the border into Scotland whenever the authorities got too close for comfort. He would often return with letters from Scottish priests which were destined for the continent; John would smuggle these on to boats sailing from Newcastle.

Unfortunately, this success meant he was greatly sought by the enemies of the Faith, especially by the Earl of Huntingdon, then Lord President of the North, who hated Catholics with a passion and had fallen into disfavour with the Government because of his failure to capture John Boste. Eventually, after many close escapes, which saw John dubbed as "one of the greatest stags in the country", John was betrayed by Francis Ecclesfield, who had told Huntingdon that he could deliver him two of the most notorious priests in the North. The traitor, Ecclesfield, had learnt that John was staying at the Warterhouse (near modern-day Esh Winning), the home of William Claxton, near Durham. This he told Huntingdon but went even further to make his plot safe by going to Communion and Confession at the house. Thus, having abused the rites of the Church and the trust of John, he met with Sir William Bowes and a group of men, leading the manhunt to John's whereabouts on 5th July, 1593.

However, John was so well hidden that the troop could not find him and thought that Ecclesfield had lied to them. Ecclesfield insisted his case though, telling them to burn down the house if necessary because he knew that the priest was in there somewhere. In response, the soldiers began to cut large chunks out of the walls and, in this way, they eventually discovered the concealed priest in a priest hole in the chimney breast.

The captured John was brought before Huntingdon, who lengthily gloated about how he had finally captured this 'evil priest' who had escaped him on numerous occasions through various cunning tricks. John was then sent to the Tower of London because of his notoriety and was cruelly racked on at least four occasions. So vicious was this torture that the unfortunate priest was crippled and forced to use a staff for the rest of his life due to the damage inflicted upon his spine. Eventually, after a harsh imprisonment, he was sent back to the North to be tried at the July assizes in 1594.

John refused to be bowed by his suffering. He was brought to trial with

*After St. John Boste had strengthened his resolve, George Swallowell died in Darlington two days after the priest, the executioner brandishing his head and proclaiming, "Behold the head of a traitor!"*

another priest (Fr. Ingram) and a former Protestant minister, George Swallowell, who had recently converted but was tempted to yield to the court's demands for conformity after a year of incarceration in Durham prison. Standing between the two priests, fearing what may happen to him, Swallowell yielded to the magistrate's demands to conform to the Church of England and all that this entailed.

At this, John turned to face Swallowell and eyed him ruefully, commenting: "George Swallowell, what hast thou done?"

At this, Swallowell began to panic. Realising the betrayal he had just committed, he pleaded with the judge and Lord President (the Earl of Huntingdon) to let him speak again, urged on by John in front of the whole court. The judge was suspicious, demanding: "Swallowell, look well what thou doest; for, although thou be condemned, yet the queen is merciful."

Taking heart from John's words and defiance, Swallowell continued to plead to be heard again, craving a chance to redeem himself. Eventually, the judge relented, commenting: "If thou be so earnest, thou shalt have thy word again; say what thou will."

Relieved at winning this reprieve, Swallowell recanted his previous weakness, saying that he would die with these priests, professing the same faith that they professed. With this, John again turned to face Swallowell and laid his hands upon the layman's head, absolving him of his momentary weakness: "Hold thee there Swallowell, and my soul for thine."

The Lord President was horrified by what he saw before him, fuming that John was reconciling Swallowell to the Roman Church. Many on the Bench jumped up and started shouting for the priest to be immediately removed and killed as a traitor. To them all, John addressed his brave reply: "My function is to invade souls, not to meddle with temporal invasions." Promptly, the court sentenced him to death on a charge of high treason because of his priesthood.

Thus, John was drawn without hesitation to the place of execution at Dryburn, just outside Durham. A huge crowd swarmed to the spot and the authorities, enraged at what had just occurred but fearful that a rescue may be attempted because of the priest's popularity, stalked the area in strength.

John recited the Angleus out loud as he climbed the gallows' ladder and had barely been turned off it to hang before he was cut down. He was still so alert that he fell to his feet but all this meant was that he was to be cruelly butchered whilst fully conscious, held in this upright position for all to see his torment. At the digging out of his heart, John was heard to cry out in a loud voice, "Jesus, Jesus, Jesus, forgive thee."

John Boste suffered on the afternoon of his trial at Durham on 24th July, 1594. George Swallowell was executed two days later in Darlington.

# Robert Southwell SJ, Tyburn, 1595

Born in 1561 to a family of good repute at the old Benedictine priory of Horsham St. Faith's in rural Norfolk, Robert Southwell was sent to Douai whilst he was still a youngster.

For some time he remained there as an alumnus of the English College at the University before making his way to Rome, where he became a Jesuit at the tender age of 17 (17th October, 1578), taking his simple vows two years later. After completing his time as a novice, and passing through his courses in philosophy and divinity with great aplomb, Robert was made Prefect of Studies in the English College of Rome after being ordained in 1584. Whilst serving in this position, he spent much time writing his famed poetry and prose.

In 1586, he was sent upon the English Mission with Fr. Henry Garnet. In England, Robert found refuge first with Lord Vaux at Harrowden before becoming chaplain to Anne Dacre, Countess of Arundel in 1588. It was here that he managed to establish relations with her husband, the imprisoned Philip, Earl of Arundel. Robert converted many during this time, including several notable names, prompting a fellow missionary Jesuit to describe him as excelling in the art "of helping and gaining souls, being at once prudent, pious, meek and exceedingly willing." Furthermore, with his fellow Jesuit Fr. Garnet, Robert gave added impetus and organisation to the Mission in the later years of Elizabeth's reign. For example, he reportedly helped to arrange a series of Mass centres, smuggled students abroad for the priesthood from a house by the river in Blackfriars, hid particularly hunted priests in Moorfields and sheltered new arrivals from the continent at a hideout in Acton. On top of all this, like Edmund Campion, he also ran a printing press, which produced his own books and poems, the latter being particularly admired in literary circles. It is also claimed that he once travelled round the country dressed as a very rich man, staying with sheriffs who felt they had to honour their distinguished guest. Little did they know that they were actually sheltering one of the most wanted priests in the land, who whilst with them was secretly administering the sacraments to Catholics in the area. It is little wonder that the pursuivants, including Cecil and Topcliffe, knew him as "the chief dealer for the papists in England." Remarkably, he had close ties with those who hounded him; Robert was a second cousin of Cecil and his mother had been governess to Queen Elizabeth!

Two letters, written to a friend in Rome, detailing the dangers of a life spent on the Mission, are presented below, underlining his poetic ability. The first one, dated 16th January, 1590, reads as follows:

"1. As yet we are alive and well, being unworthy, it seems, of prisons. We have oftener sent than received letters from your parts, though they are not sent without difficulty, and some we know have been lost.

2. The condition of Catholic recusants here is the same as usual, deplorable and full of fears and dangers, more especially since our adversaries have looked for war. As many of ours as are in chains rejoice and are comforted in their prisons, and they that are at liberty set not their hearts upon it, nor expect it to be of long continuance. All, by the great goodness and mercy of God, arm themselves to suffer anything that can come, how hard soever it may be, as it shall please our Lord, for whose greater glory and the salvation of their souls they are more concerned than for any temporal losses.

3. A little while ago they apprehended two priests, who have suffered such cruel usages in the prison of Bridewell as can scarcely be believed. What was given them to eat was so little in quantity, and withal so filthy and nauseous that the very sight of it was enough to turn their stomachs. The labours to which they obliged them were continual and immoderate, and no less in sickness than in health; for with hard blows and stripes they forced them to accomplish their task, how weak soever they were. Their beds were dirty straw, and their prison most filthy.

4. Some are there hung up for whole days by the hands, in such manner that they can but just touch the ground with the tips of their toes. In fine, that they are kept in that prison truly live *in lacu miseria et in luto facis*, Psalm xxxix. This purgatory we are looking for every hour, in which Topcliffe and Young, the two executioners of the Catholics, exercise all kinds of torments. But come what pleaseth God, we hope we shall be able to bear all in Him that strengthens us. In the meantime we pray that they may be put to confusion who work iniquity, and that the Lord may speak peace to His people, Psalms xxiv and lxxxiv, that, as the royal prophet says, His glory may dwell in our land. I most humbly recommend myself to the holy sacrifices of your reverence and of all our friends."

The second is dated 8th March, 1590:

"1. We have written many letters, but it seems few have come to your hands. We sail in the midst of these stormy waves with no small danger, from which, nevertheless, it has pleased our Lord hitherto to deliver us.

2. We have altogether, with much comfort, renewed

the vows of the Society, according to our custom, spending some days in exhortations and spiritual conferences. *Aperuimus ora et attraximus spiritum*. It seems to me that I see the beginnings of a religious life set on foot in England, of which we now sow the seeds with tears, that others hereafter may with joy carry in the sheaves to the heavenly granaries.

3. We have sung the canticles of the Lord in a strange land, and in this desert we have sucked honey from the rock and oil from the hard stone. But these our joys ended in sorrow, and sudden fears dispersed us into different places; but, in fine, we were more afraid than hurt, for we all escaped. I , with another of ours, seeking to avoid Scylla, had like to have fallen into Charybdis; but, by the mercy of God, we passed betwixt them both without being shipwrecked, and are now sailing in a safe harbour.

4. In another of mine, I gave account of the late martyrdoms of Mr. Bale and Mr. Horner, and of the edification which the people received from their holy ends. With such dews as these the Church is watered, *ut in stillicidiis hujusmodi latetur germinans*, Psalm lxiv. We also look for the time (if we are not unworthy of so great a glory) when our day, like that of the hired servant, shall come. In the meanwhile I recommend myself very much to your reverence's prayers, that the Father of Lights may enlighten us, and confirm us with His principle Spirit."

Robert's day came on 20th June, 1592, when he was betrayed by a girl named Anne Bellamy and apprehended in her father's house at Uxendon Hall in Harrow, Middlesex, just outside London. Topcliffe was the joyous captor, excitingly informing the queen, "I never did take so weighty a man, if he be rightly used." Robert was thrown into a dungeon in the Tower that was so filthy that when he emerged at the end of the month to be examined, his clothes were covered in vermin, lice and dirt.

Upon this, Robert's father presented a petition to the queen begging that if his son had done anything that deserved death, then he should suffer but if he had not, he hoped that Her Majesty would order his son to be treated as a gentleman and not confined any longer in that filthy hole. The queen promptly ordered that Robert be kept in a better holding place and that the guards should allow his father to supply him with clothes and other necessities. The books that the priest requested were also to be delivered - the Holy Bible and the works of St. Bernard.

Robert was imprisoned for three years and cruelly questioned under torture 13 times. Topcliffe even experimented with a special new torture on the unfortunate priest, hanging him by the hands for so many hours that he eventually began to vomit blood. However, Robert refused to crack even under these severe pressures, revealing noth-

ing to his persecutors. Finally, the Privy Council adopted a resolution that he should be brought to trial.

Some days before his hearing, Robert was moved to Newgate prison, where he was cast into a notorious dungeon called 'Limbo'. His trial was on 22nd February, 1595. Given no prior notice of it, so unable to prepare in any way, Robert was hurried to Westminster. The judges before whom he was brought were Lord Chief-Justice Popham, Justice Owen, Baron Evans, and Sergeant Daniel. The Lord Chief-Justice started proceedings with a lengthy and vehement denunciation of the Jesuits and seminary priests, claiming that they were behind multitudes of plots and conspiracies against the queen. The indictment against Robert was then read, before he was ordered to approach the bar and enter his plea:

"I confess that I was born in England, a subject to the Queen's Majesty, and that by authority derived from God I have been promoted to the sacred order of priesthood in the Roman Church, for which I return most hearty thanks to His Divine Majesty. I confess also that I was at Uxendon, in Middlesex, at that time when, being sent for thither by trick and deceit, I fell into your hands, as it is well known. But that I never entertained any designs or plots against the queen or kingdom, I call God to witness, the revenger of perjury; neither had I any other design in returning home to my native country than to administer the sacraments according to the rite of the Catholic Church to such as desired them."

Having had enough of this lengthy dictate, the judges ordered him to just proffer a simple plea to which Robert responded by saying he was not guilty of any treason. Although at first arguing that the laws of the land were against those of God, so he would not be tried by them, Robert eventually relented. Thus, they went about proving the priest's guilt. When asked his age, Robert replied that he was 33, the same as Jesus, drawing much rebuke from his accusers. The priest shirked off their criticisms, responding that he was not claiming to be equal to Jesus for he was but a worm in comparison. Duly, Robert was found guilty, prompting him to bow before the bar, thanking them for the great service they had done him.

On 21st February 1595, only the day after he was condemned, Robert was brought for execution at Tyburn. Great care was taken not to let the people know he was to be executed that day so that the route to the gallows would not be blocked. A famous highwayman was to be executed at the same time in a different place in an attempt to lure away the crowds. However, these attempts failed miserably and people packed the route, including a number of notable figures.

After reaching the execution place, Robert rose from his hurdle and climbed on to the cart under the noose. Despite his hands being tied, he made the Sign of the Cross as best he could, and started to talk to the assembled mass.

*continues on page 50*

"Whether we live, we live to the Lord: or whether we die, we die to the Lord. Therefore, whether we live or die, we belong to the Lord."

The Sheriff tried to stop him but Robert pleaded that he be allowed to continue, promising to say nothing inflammatory.

"I am come to this place to finish my course, and to pass out of this miserable life, and I beg of my Lord Jesus Christ, in whose most precious passion and blood I place my hope of salvation, that He would have mercy on my soul. I confess I am a Catholic priest of the Holy Roman Church, and a religious man of the Society of Jesus, on which account I owe eternal thanks and praise to my God and Saviour."

At this point, a minister interjected, claiming that this was damnable doctrine but the crowd bayed for silence, wishing the condemned priest to continue.

"Sir, I beg of you not to be troublesome to me for this short time that I have to live. I am a Catholic, and in whatever manner you may please to interpret my words, I hope for salvation by the merits of our Lord Jesus Christ. And as to the Queen, I never attempted nor contrived or imagined any evil against her, but have always prayed for her to Our Lord; and for this short time of my life still pray that, in His infinite mercy, He would be pleased to give her all such gifts and graces which He sees in His divine wisdom to be most expedient for the welfare both of her soul and body, in this life and in the next. I recommend, in like manner, to the same mercy of God my poor country, and I implore the Divine bounty to favour it with His light and the knowledge of His truth, to the greater advancement of the salvation of souls, and the eternal glory of His Divine Majesty. In fine, I beg of the Almighty and Everlasting God, that this, my death, may be for my own and for my country's good, and the comfort of the Catholics my brethren."

Finishing, Robert blessed himself, raised his eyes to heaven, and uttered the following words in Latin, "Into thy hands, O Lord, I commend my Spirit." With that, the cart was drawn away.

However, the hangman was unskilled and so had applied the noose around the wrong part of the neck. Thus, Robert hanged for a great length of time, being slowly strangled, several times making the Sign of the Cross. Some seeing this brutal torture began to pull the priest's legs to try and quicken his release. When the executioner went to cut the rope whilst he was still alive, the crowd shouted their disapproval, including the Protestants present who were greatly affected by the priest's dignity during the gruesome act. When the 33 year-old Robert was finally dead, his body was cut down, disembowelled and quartered.

Henry Walpole, born in 1558, was the eldest of a large family of boys from Docking, Norfolk. Entering Peterhouse, Cambridge, in 1575, he went on to study law in London at Gray's Inn in 1578. Witnessing the martyrdom of Edmund Campion and being spattered by the priest's blood, Henry converted to Catholicism. During this time, he read widely about his new religion so that he was able to defend it against any attacks and even win many converts. In time, this brought the Government's attention upon him, particularly after he wrote a widely circulated poem about Edmund Campion (see later). Thus, he decided to follow his conscience and fled to the English College, then based at Rheims.

Arriving on 7th July, 1582, the Douai Diary records it thus: "*7 die Julij ex Anglia ad nos venit D. Henricus Walpole, vir discretus, gravis et pius*" (On the 7th July Mr. Henry Walpole came to us out of England, a discreet, grave, and pious man). He remained at the college for a year before being sent to the college at Rome with four others, where he entered into the Society of Jesus on 28th April 1583. After completing his studies, Henry was ordained in Paris on 15th December, 1588. Three of his brothers shortly followed suit, and a fourth went abroad to serve as an officer in the Spanish forces in the Netherlands.

Henry's health declined while he was in Italy, so his superiors sent him to Pont-a-Mousson in Lorraine, before he continued into Flanders. It was here in 1589, whilst travelling on foot and acting as a chaplain to the multi-national force serving under the Prince of Palma in Belgium, that he fell into the hands of a party of Calvinists then fighting against the force. They took him prisoner and he was incarcerated at Flushing for a whole year before one of his brothers eventually procured his liberty. However, this suffering further spurred him on, provoking a fire within him to be sent to England and win conversions, as well as the crown of martyrdom. His superiors would not assent to his desires though, instead sending him to two new English seminaries recently set up in Spain. He was vice-rector at Seville, before staying longer in the same position at Valladolid. From there, he returned to Flanders with a commission from the King of Spain to the Council for the establishment of another English seminary at St. Omer.

Eventually, he was given permission to head for England. He was set ashore at Bridlington, Yorkshire on the night of 6th December, 1593. Only 24 hours passed before he was caught by the authorities, along with his two companions, at Killam. Three days later, he was carried as a prisoner to York. The Earl of Huntingdon, then Lord President of the North, examined him, along with the rest of the Council of the North, and Henry freely admitted that he was a priest. Upon this, he was committed to York gaol as a close prisoner until 25th February 1594, when the Privy Council ordered him to be sent to London.

After his capture, Henry sent a letter to a Fr. Richard, a fellow Jesuit and missionary in Yorkshire:

"Although your reverence has subscribed no name to your letter, I plainly understand it is from a friend and from a fellow-soldier, which gives me a very great comfort. I should be overjoyed if I could confer with your reverence by word of mouth about certain concerns of mine. In the meantime, most dear father, I recommend myself to your holy prayers, and those of the rest of our brethren and friends in Christ Jesus our Lord. I know not as yet what will become of me; but whatever shall happen, by the face of God it shall be welcome; for in every place, north or south, east or west, He is at hand; and the wings of His protection and government are stretched forth to every place where they are who truly serve and worship Him, and study to promote the glory and honour of His most holy and most precious name. I trust that He will be glorified in me, whether in life or death, *qui capit perficict; mihi vivere Christus est et mori lucrum*. Some come to dispute with me, but with clamours and empty words more than with solid arguments. I cannot go on, *custos adest*. I recommend your reverence to our guardian angel, and to the whole court of heaven, and (above all) to our Lord Jesus Christ. *Memento mei*."

On reaching the capital, Henry was imprisoned in the Tower for a year. During his time there, he was tortured no less than 14 times, as he himself would confirm a little before his death. The carvings that he made on the wall of his cell can still be seen in the Salt Tower – "IHS", "Maria", Christ's nail-pierced hands and feet, and His stricken heart. Details of his questioning by Topcliffe whilst under torture are contained in another letter sent to 'Fr. Richard'.

"Your reverence's letters give me great comfort; but if I could but see you, though it were but for one hour, it would be of greater service to me than I could possibly express. I hope that what is wanting my sweet Lord Jesus will supply by other means, whose heavenly comfort and assistance has always hitherto stood by me in my greatest necessities, and I am persuaded will continue to do so, since His love for us is everlasting.

"If I would write down all things that have here passed with our adversaries it would be endless, and the work of a long time. In my examination I give in writing a long account of my life beyond the seas, of the places where I lived, and of my actions and designs, which, I assured them, had no other end than only the glory of God, and the increase of the holy Catholic faith. With which view I told them I returned to England, with a very great desire of the conversion of the people, but most of all of the queen herself, and of the whole English nobility, which I plainly assured them I should ever use my best endeavours to bring about with the grace of God.

"To their queries concerning others, I refused to answer. And when Topcliffe threatened that he would make me answer when he had me in Bridewell or in the Tower, I told him that our Lord God, I hoped, would never permit me, for fear of any torments whatsoever, to do anything against his Divine Majesty, or against my own conscience, or to the prejudice of justice and the innocence of others.

"I have had various conferences and disputations with many of the heretics. And whereas I believed I should have been tried at the last assizes in this city, "York," I sent in writing to the Lord President all those conferences and disputations, who had ordered me pen, ink and paper for that purpose. To which I joined a large discourse or treatise, in which I exhorted all to beware of false prophets, and to give ear to the voice of the Holy Church, the spouse of the king, the house, the vineyard, and the city of Christ. One of the ministers complained of me much to the president for being so bold as to put down such things in writing, but he could not refute what was written; and, indeed, they seem to me to be much confounded. Blessed be Jesus, *qui dat os insipienti, cui non possunt resistere sapientes*. I want very much to have a book or two for a few hours; but if I cannot have them, Jesus, our God and Lord, is at hand, and He is the Eternal Wisdom. Your reverence will be pleased to pray to Him that He may always stand by me, and so that all things may turn out to His glory.

"I am much astonished that so vile a creature as I am should be so near, as they tell me, to the crown of martyrdom; but this I know for certain, that the blood of my most Blessed Saviour and Redeemer, and His most sweet love, is able to make me worthy of it, *omnia possum in eo qui me comfortat*. Your reverence, most loving Father, is engaged in the midst of the battle. I sit here an idle spectator of the field; yet King David has appointed an equal portion for us both, and love, charity, and union, which united us together in Jesus Christ Our Lord, make us mutually partakers of one another's merits; and what can be more closely united than we two, who, as your reverence sees, *simul segregati sumus in hoc ministerium*.

"The president inquired of me who was the superior of our Society in this kingdom, whether it was this or the other, or who it was? Topcliffe answered he knew who it was, and named him. I beg your reverence would communicate this letter to all our friends. I desire to give myself to every one of them, and more particularly to all our most dear fathers and brothers of the Society of Christ my Jesus, in whose prayers, labours, and sacrifices, as I have a share, so have I a great confidence. About mid-Lent I hope my lot will be decided, either for life or death; for then the assizes will be held here again. In the meanwhile I have leisure to prepare myself, and expect with good courage whatever His Divine Majesty shall be pleased to appoint for me. I beg your reverence to join your holy prayers with my poor ones, that I may walk worthy of that high and holy name and profession to which I am called, which I trust in the mercy of our Lord He will grant me, not regarding so much my many imperfections as the fervent labours, prayers, and holy sacrifices of so many fathers, and my brothers His servants, who are employed over all the world in His service; and I hope, through the merits

*continues on page 52*

of my most sweet Saviour and Lord, that I shall be always ready, whether living or dying, to glorify Him, which will be for my eternal happiness. And if my unworthiness and demerits shall keep me at present at a distance from the crown, I will strive to deserve it by a greater solicitude and diligence for the future; and if, in His mercy, our Lord shall grant me now to wash my garments in the blood of the Lamb, I hope to follow Him for ever, clothed in white.

"I can never end when I get any time to write to your reverence, which I have been seldom able to do; and whether, as long as I live, I shall ever have another opportunity, I know not. I confessed in my examinations that I had laboured for the increase of the two seminaries in Spain, and for that of St. Omer's, and that I had returned hearty thanks to his Catholic Majesty for his great favours to the seminary of St. Omer's. I also confessed that all my actions had always in view the good of others, and no one's harm; the procuring peace among all, and the propagating our holy Catholic faith and the kingdom of Christ to the utmost of my power. This was the sum of my general confession which I gave in writing, signed by my own hand, the president and to Topcliffe. They asked me what would I do if the Pope should wage war against England. I answered that the circumstances of that time would give me more light, and that I should then have recourse to our Lord God for counsel, and would think seriously on it before I would anyways intermeddle with things of war. *Haec et hujusmodi, de quibus postea.* May Jesus be always with your reverence. *Oremus pro invicem.*"

After the year had passed, Henry was sent back to York in the Spring of 1595 for his trial. He opened proceedings with a declaration of his innocence in relation to the charges against him.

"I find, my Lords, I am accused of two or three things. First, that I am a priest, ordained by the authority of the See of Rome. Secondly, that I am a Jesuit, or one of the Society of Jesus. Thirdly, that I returned to my country to exercise the ordinary acts of these two callings, which are no other than to gain souls to God. I will show that none of these things can be treason. Not the being a priest, which is a dignity and office instituted by our Lord Jesus Christ, and given by Him to His apostles, who were priests, as were also the holy fathers and doctors of the Church who converted and instructed the world, and the first teachers who brought over the English nation to the light of the Gospel were also priests; so that were it not for priests we should all be heathens, consequently to be a priest can be no treason."

Judge Beaumont then spoke: "Indeed, the merely being a priest or Jesuit is no treason; but what makes you a traitor is your returning into the kingdom against the laws."

"If to be a priest," replied Henry, "is no treason, the executing the office or doing the functions of a priest can be no treason."

The judge pondered this argument. "But if a priest should conspire against the person of his prince, would not this be treason?

"Yes, but then neither his being a priest nor the following the duties of his calling would make him a traitor, but the committing to a crime contrary to the duty of a priest, which is far from being my case," responded Henry.

"You have been," claimed the judge, "with the King of Spain, and you have treated and conversed with [Frs.] Parsons and Holt, and other rebels and traitors to the kingdom; and you have returned hither contrary to the laws, and therefore you cannot deny your being a traitor."

Henry was not deterred: "To speak or treat with any person whatsoever out of the kingdom can make me no traitor, as long as no proof can be brought that the subject about which we treated was treason; neither can the returning to my native country be looked upon as treason, since the cause of my return was not to do any evil, either to the Queen or to the kingdom."

"Our laws appoint," pronounced the judge grandly, "that a priest who returns from beyond the seas, and does not present himself before a justice within three days to make the usual submission to the Queen's Majesty in matters of religion, shall be deemed a traitor."

"Then I am out of the case, who was apprehended before I had been one whole day on English ground," came Henry's triumphant reply.

Judge Beaumont was taken aback, aware that he had been roundly defeated. Judge Elvin stepped into the breach though and asked Henry if he was ready to proclaim his submission to the queen in matters of religion as required by law, along with acknowledging her supremacy and renouncing the Pope.

The priest's reply was unflinching; he did not know what laws they had made in England whilst he was abroad, nor what submissions these laws required. However, he did know that no man-made law could make him do anything contrary to the law of God, and that submission to earthly princes must always be subordinate to that given to God. He went even further:

"You, my Lords, sit here at present in judgment as men, and judge as such, being subject to error and passion, but know for certain that there is a Sovereign Judge who will judge righteously, whom in all things we must obey in the first place, and then our lawful princes in such things as are lawful, and no further."

The Lord President could not stay quiet at such provocation. "We deal very favourably with you, Mr Walpole, when, notwithstanding all these treasons and conspiracies with the persons aforesaid, we offer you the benefit of the law if you will but make the submission ordered by the law, which, if you will not accept of, it is proper you should be punished according to the law.

Henry replied as follows: "There is nothing, my Lord, in which I would not most willingly submit myself, provided it be not against God; but may his Divine Majesty never suffer me to consent to the least thing by which He may be dishonoured, nor you to desire it of me. As to the queen, I every day pray for her to our Lord God that He would bless her with His Holy Spirit, and give her His grace to do her duty in all things in this world, to the end that she may enjoy eternal glory in the world to come; and God is my witness that to all here present, and particularly to my accusers and such as desire my death, I wish as to myself the salvation of their souls, and that to the end they may live in the true Catholic faith, the only way to eternal happiness."

The court, fearing the crowd's reaction to these words, for by this time they could not help but see that the charge of treason against the priest was but a pretence when a submission to the queen's religion was all that was insisted upon, decided to finish the trial. Thus, the judge summarised the evidence against the prisoner, which was nothing more than Henry's own confession : that he was a priest and a Jesuit; that he had been with the King of Spain; that he had treated with Fr. Parsons and Fr. Holt, and others whom they called fugitives, rebels and traitors, and that he had returned into England to convert his country, or as they interpreted it, to seduce her Majesty's subjects from the religion established by law, and to reconcile them to the See of Rome.

The jury was then directed to find him guilty of the indictment. Henry addressed the jury as they were departing: "Gentlemen of the jury, I confess most willingly that I am a priest, and that I am of the Company of Jesus or a Jesuit, and that I came over in order to convert my country to the Catholic faith, and to invite sinners to repentance. All this I will never deny; this is the duty of my calling. If you find anything else in me that is not agreeable to my profession, show me no favour. In the meantime, act according to your consciences, and remember you must give an account to God."

Returning very quickly, the jury duly pronounced Henry as guilty. He was promptly sentenced to death for being a priest - high treason at the time. The jury pronounced him guilty on 3rd April and he received his sentence on the 5th. He was advised to prepare for death two days later.

The events surrounding his treatment in the Tower and return to York are detailed in a letter from Fr. Henry Garnet, the Superior of the English Jesuits, dated 23rd October, 1595:

"Blessed Father Walpole met in the Tower of London with the greatest misery and poverty, so that the Lieutenant himself, though otherwise a hard-hearted and barbarous man, was moved to inquire after some of the Father's relations, and told them that he was in great and extraordinary want - without bed, without clothes, without anything to cover him, and that at a season when the cold was most sharp and piercing, so that himself, though an enemy, out of pure compassion had given him a little straw to sleep on. Besides this, the Father himself in public court, upon occasion of answering some question that was put to him, declared that he had been tortured 14 times; and it is very well known how cruel any one of those tortures is which are now in use. For it is a common thing to hang them up in the air six or seven hours by the hands, and, by means of certain irons, which hold their hands fast and cut them, they shed much blood in the torture. The force of this torment may be gathered from what happened last Lent to a laic called James Atkinson, whom they most cruelly tortured in this manner to oblige him to accuse his own master and other Catholics and

priests, and kept him so long in the torture that he was at length taken away for dead after many hours' suffering, and, in effect, died within two hours. Some time after they carried the Father back to York, to be tried at the mid-Lent assizes. In all that journey he never went into bed, or even lay down upon a bed to rest himself after the fatigue of the day, but his sleep was upon the bare ground. When he came to York, he was put into prison, where he waited many days for the judges coming [sic]. In the prison he had nothing but one poor mat three feet long, on which he made his prayer upon his knees for a great part of the night; and when he slept, it was upon the ground, leaning upon the same mat. And besides this long prayer in the night, which lasted for the greater part of the night, he spent not a little time in making English verses, in which he had a particular talent and grace; for before he left the kingdom, he had made a poem upon the martyrdom of Father Campion, which was so much taken notice of by the public, that, the author not being known, the gentleman who published it was condemned by the Council to lose his ears and to pass the remainder of his days in prison, in which, after some years, he made a pious end." [It is of note that the poem was so notorious that 13 years later, an Essex farmer was charged for possessing a copy in his own handwriting!]

On the morning of 7th April, the condemned priest was drawn with Fr. Alexander Rawlins to the place of execution at Knavesmire, just outside the city of York. Fr. Rawlins suffered first, and Henry was made to watch his companion being quartered. The authorities bade him to show more wisdom than Fr. Rawlins, offering him his life if he conformed. Henry rejected their bribes and mounted the ladder. As he climbed, they pressed him further, asking what he thought of the queen's spiritual supremacy. When he declared that he was against it, they howled that this was treason before calling for him to pray with them so that he would die in peace. The defiant reply came that, through the grace of God, he was at peace with the world, and prayed for everyone, especially those who had played a role in bringing about his death. Moreover, they were not of his faith so he would not pray with them but heartily prayed for them; that God would enlighten them with His truth, bringing them back to the Catholic Church. Begging the prayers of all Catholics there present, he lifted up his hands and eyes to heaven and said the Lord's Prayer. Starting the Angelic Salutation, the persecutors ordered him to be pushed off the ladder before he had even finished.

However, the rope was quickly cut. Thus, Henry was fully conscious as he was dismembered, disembowelled and quartered. Many spectators were traumatised by the sight, and his death served as a great boost to the Church in the North.

Henry Walpole was executed at York on 7th April, 1595. The Earl of Huntingdon, the great persecutor of the Northern Catholics, did not survive the year. He died in a much-troubled state of conscience, calling often for his brother, the most Honourable Walter Hastings. His brother, a devout Catholic, did not arrive in time though, and Huntingdon died as a Protestant.

*The Duke of Norfolk, related to St. Philip Howard, leaves St. Peter's Basilica after attending the canonisation by Pope Paul VI of the Forty Martyrs of England and Wales.*

# Philip Howard, layman, London, 1595

**B**orn at Arundel House in London on 28th June, 1557, Philip was the grandson of the poet Henry Howard, Earl of Surrey, who had been executed under Henry VIII in 1547, and the son of Thomas Howard, Duke of Norfolk, who Elizabeth I had executed in 1572 for his alleged involvement in the Ridolfi Plot and with Mary, Queen of Scots. Furthermore, Philip II of Spain, who was, at the time of Philip's birth, King of England, was the young Howard's godson at his baptism performed by Nicholas Heath, Archbishop of York, in the chapel of Whitehall Palace. This underlines that the persecution of Catholics knew no bounds and was heedless of family contacts and social status.

Philip's father, who conformed to the State religion, had him educated partly under John Foxe, the famous Protestant martyrologist, and he was raised as a Protestant despite being baptised a Catholic. Subsequently, Philip was sent to St. John's College, Cambridge University, from which he graduated in 1574, but not before, as a 14 year-old, he had married Anne Dacre, Countess of Arundel and Surrey, after his father had taken his third wife, Anne's widowed mother, Elizabeth. In fact, each of Thomas Howard's three sons was married to his new wife's daughters, who all just happened to be heiresses! Anne was noted for her generosity and courage, and after her conversion she became the patroness of, amongst other priests, Fr. Robert Southwell and founded the Jesuit novitiate in Ghent.

On 24th February, 1580, Philip succeeded his father as Earl of Arundel. Frequenting the Court, the handsome, witty, good dancer began to gain favour with Elizabeth, entertaining her at his residence. Subsequently, he was restored 'in blood' in 1581, though not to his father's dukedom. Like many of Elizabeth's courtiers at the time, he was not necessarily that well behaved, being indifferent to his faith and embarking on numerous affairs whilst his wife stayed at home.

However, towards the end of the year, Philip was present during Edmund Campion's staged disputations and these began to bear heavily on his mind. The Howards had enemies and Philip was rapidly falling from the queen's favour due to a number of circumstances. As Catholicism failed to disappear and even began winning converts through the work of the missionaries, the earl found himself out of favour and under suspicion because of his family's history. When his wife converted with Philip's favourite sister, Lady Margaret Sackville, Anne was banished from court and placed under house arrest in Surrey, where she gave birth to their daughter, Elizabeth. The suspicion intensified and Philip was imprisoned in the Tower of London for a short time. However, as mentioned, he had begun to turn towards Catholicism after witnessing the treatment of Edmund Campion and hearing the martyr's arguments. This had already led to reconciliation with, and new devotion to, his wife, and on his release from the Tower, he followed her into the Catholic Church on 30th September, 1584. He was received into the Faith by the Jesuit priest William Weston and from that day on was fervent in his Catholicism.

Of course, this change in lifestyle did not go un-noticed. With the queen becoming colder and colder towards him, utterings being made in Court and laws against Catholics being stringently enforced, Philip decided that it was time to leave the country. Before he departed England, the earl wrote an eloquent letter to Elizabeth explaining his actions. Stating that it was to be delivered to her after he had gone, he indicated that he was leaving the country for the safety of his soul and the service of God, but not leaving behind his loyalty to, and affection for, the queen.

Betrayed by one of his servants, Philip was arrested at sea on 14th April, 1585, whilst aboard the ship that he thought would take him to safety. He was brought back to London and incarcerated in the Tower of London on 25th April. Severely beaten, he was accused of treason for working with Mary, Queen of Scots. All those with him at the time, including his brother William, uncle, friends and servants were also arrested and sent to several different prisons. The wretched earl was to be imprisoned at the queen's pleasure and fined the massive sum of ten thousand pounds despite no evidence being produced against him.

After four years or so of prison, in the wake of the rabid anti-Catholicism that followed the failed Spanish Armada, Philip was again brought to trial before the King's Bench under the guise that new evidence had come to light. On 4th April, 1589, the prisoner was sentenced to death for having supported the queen's excommunication and for having prayed for the success of the Spanish Armada. As usual, the trial was a travesty. For example, existing State Papers show that the vicious Catholic persecutor Attorney-General Popham was well aware that the evidence brought against Philip was fraudulent. Philip valiantly defend-

ed himself and his defence is summed up in the declaration he later penned to be read before his execution: "For the satisfaction of all men and discharge of my conscience before God, I here protest before His Divine Majesty and all the Holy Court of Heaven, that I have committed no treason, and that the Catholic and Roman faith, which I hold, is the only cause (so far as I can in any way imagine) why either I have been thus long imprisoned, or for which I am now ready to be executed."

However, Philip was not executed; instead, he was left to die a painful lingering death - possibly worse than the immediate end that was brought by execution – wondering each day if that was the one on which he was to die. He was kept as a close prisoner for ten years in total, during which time he led a devout life of regular prayer and contemplation, which led him to pen several religious works that were printed after his death. He was also known to fast on bread and water alone for three days of each week, as well as being patient in his suffering and courteous to even the rudest of guards. Furthermore, he regularly performed acts of penance, particularly for the manner in which he had previously treated his wife. His final wish was to see his wife and only son, Thomas, who had been born just after Philip's imprisonment. This small desire was denied unless he would conform, on which occasion his freedom would also be granted.

Refusing to compromise till the end and weakened by severe malnutrition, Philip, Earl of Arundel, died at the age of 38 on 19th October, 1595, after a night of continuous prayer. There were, and still are, strong suspicions and persistent rumours that he was actually poisoned, as the symptoms of his final illness were consistent with that fate. He was buried in the Tower Church in the same grave as his grandfather and father. In 1624, his remains were removed by his widow and taken to Long Horsely, before they were finally interred in the

Fitzalan Chapel in Arundel. Finally, in 1971, his remains were enshrined in Arundel Cathedral.

Over the fireplace in his cell in the Beauchamp Tower of the Tower of London, Philip carved the following in Latin, which can still be seen today:

"The more affliction we endure for Christ in this world, the more glory we shall obtain with Christ in the next – Arundell, Jun 22, 1587."

# John Jones OFM, Southwark, 1598

John Jones (also known as Buckley) was born into a Catholic gentleman's family in the parish of Clynog Fawr, Caernarvonshire. Little is known of his youth.

He entered the Franciscan convent at Greenwich, which was dissolved in 1559. From there he went to the continent, and was professed at Pontoise, France. He subsequently returned to England to labour as a secular priest amongst the prisoners in Marshalsea prison but was discovered and incarcerated at Wisbeach Castle in 1587. In time, he managed to escape abroad and journeyed to Rome, where he stayed at the Ara Coeli Franciscan Observant house. Shortly after he joined the Roman province of the reformed Franciscan order of Strict Observance in 1591, one of the strictest religious orders and the first to be suppressed by King Henry VIII. Fully enrolled, John begged to be allowed to go upon the English Mission. Permission granted, he received a special blessing and commendation from Pope Clement VIII.

He returned to England some time between late 1592 and early 1593. Initially, he stayed at the house established in London for missionary priests by Fr. John Gerard but soon headed out to different parts of the country for his labours. During this time, his fellow Franciscans elected him as their provincial.

After three years of striving around the London area with great success, he was captured for a final time in 1596 and imprisoned for two years on the evidence of the infamous Topcliffe. A spy informed Topcliffe that John had visited two Catholics and had said Mass in their house, but it was afterwards shown that these people were in prison when the alleged offence took place. After being arrested, John was mercilessly tortured; this included the horror of being scourged. Moreover, Topcliffe brought him to his house and practised other unspeakable barbarities upon the indefatigable priest. During his incarceration, many people visited him and learnt from his words till Topcliffe eventually caused him to be charged along with Robert Barnes and Jane Wiseman (who had both been helping him during his labours, Mrs. Wiseman nursing John when he developed a painful ulcer on his leg) on 3rd July, 1598. John pleaded that he was guilty of no crime against the queen or country and requested that his case be considered by the judges rather than an ignorant jury. Judge Clinch informed him that they were well aware he was no plotter against the queen but was a Catholic priest who had stayed in the country against the laws, which was decreed as high treason.

"If this be a crime, I must own myself guilty, for I am a priest, and came over into England to gain as many souls as I could to Christ," replied John defiantly.

Thus, he was sentenced to the usual punishment of death. Falling to his knees, the priest gave thanks to God in a loud voice. Mr. Barnet and Mrs. Wiseman were also sentenced to death but they were later spared.

Early on the morning of 12th July, John was drawn to St. Thomas' Waterings (now the Old Kent Road), the place designated for execution. Having been taken off the sledge and pushed up into the cart under the gallows, he declared that he had never spoken a word or entertained a thought against the queen or his country. Rather, he professed to the remarkably large crowd despite the hour, that he prayed for their welfare daily.

John was made to wait for an hour in this position as the hangman had forgotten the rope. During this prolonged torture, he spent the time praying and preaching before the rope was finally brought and placed around his neck. With that, the cart was quickly drawn away and the priest was hanged until he was dead.

Once cut down, his body was disembowelled and quartered, his quarters set on poles on the roads to Newington and Lambeth, whilst his head was displayed in Southwark. Catholics later recovered his body parts despite the danger; at least two of the protagonists were caught and imprisoned for attempting this act.

John Jones suffered on the summer morning of 12th July, 1598, in Southwark. Fr. Henry Garnet wrote an account of his life only three days after the martyr's death.

# John Rigby, layman, London, 1600

Born around 1570, John Rigby was the youngest son of Nicholas Rigby, a gentleman from a long-established family who lived at Harrocks Hall in Eccleston, Lancashire. Initially, John was a church papist, sometimes attending Protestant services despite being Catholic at heart. He later repented of this, confessing to Fr. John Jones during the Franciscan priest's time in prison. Reconciled to the Church, John lived an exemplary life from that time, converting many to the Church, including his aged father.

Whilst John was in the service of the strict Protestant Sir Edmund Huddleston, the latter's daughter, the widowed Mrs. Fortescue, was summoned to the sessions on charges of recusancy. Unable to attend due to illness, she asked John to go in her place to testify for her in court.

Unfortunately, one of the commissioners, Sir Richard Martin, held a deep dislike of John and began to question him about his own religion instead of Mrs. Fortescue's. Knowing that John would not deny his faith, Sir Richard was able to prove that John was Catholic and refused to attend the Protestant services. Moreover, he refused to take the oath of the queen's supremacy, resulting in the lord mayor and the other commissioners sending him to Newgate prison.

The following day (14th February, 1600), he was again examined, this time by the Lord Chief-Justice. Once more, John professed his faith and admitted that he used to conform despite always being a Catholic. However, he continued, he realised that such a practice was inconsistent with Catholicism and he had been reconciled by Fr. John Jones whilst in the Clink, and for the two or three years since that day, he had not set foot in a Protestant church. At some point during his internment John was tortured in an attempt to make him reveal more details about Catholics in England. He was lowered on to what could best be described as an open heated oven, the bars scorching and burning his flesh. At the same time, a barber was ordered to shave the poor man's head but John remained amazingly defiant, paying the barber for the hair cut, later writing, "Whereat there was great laughing and I not the least merry, I am sure"!

John recorded what followed, including his trial at the Surrey Sessions House in Southwark, whilst he was in prison and sent the testimony to a friend for safekeeping:

"Then my lord commanded the keeper to take me and to put on me an iron chain, which, when it came, I willed him to put it on in God's name, and said aloud, 'I would not change my chain for my lord mayor's great chain'; and I gave the fellow sixpence for his pains.

"By-and-by my Lord Chief-Justice sent me word to provide myself, for I was to be arraigned forthwith. I bid the messenger tell his lordship I never heard so good news in my life before; and so I was commanded to the common gaol. But, expecting every day to be arraigned, the Tuesday following I was removed to the White Lion in Southwark, and was there quiet till 3rd March. [It was actually 4th March, not 3rd as John believed]

"And Wednesday 3rd March, in the common sessions, with a number of felons I was brought to my trial. In the forenoon I was called and appeared,

but nothing was said to me. When the justice went to dinner we also went home to prison; and being at dinner, Justice Gaudy sent his man for me, and I went willingly with my keeper; and so coming to them at Justice Dale's house, where the judges dined, Justice Gaudy called me to him and asked my name, which I told him.

'Were not you committed by Lord Chief-Justice and examined by him?'

'Yes, my lord.'

'You know your own hand?' so he showed me my hand.

'This is my hand. I pray you give me leave to speak for myself.'

'You shall. I well perceive you have thought better of the matter. I am told by one of my Lord of Canterbury's gentlemen that you are now sorry for what you have done, and willing to become a good subject and go to church. If you will so do, her Majesty is merciful. How say you? Will you go to church now?'

'No, my lord. Good, my lord, whosoever informed your lordship that ever I did yet yield in any point of my profession was not my friend, nor ever had my consent thereto. I assure you, my lord, I am a true subject, and obedient to her Majesty and her laws in anything which may not hurt my conscience; but to say that I will go to church, I never will. Yea, rather than you lordships should have any light suspicion of me of such a consent, take my first answer as it is; there is my hand, here is my whole body, and most ready I am and willing to seal it with my blood.'

'We were told,' said one of the judges, 'you were a simple young man, and willing to recant, but law must proceed.'

'Let me have law, in the name of Jesus. God's will be done.'

"The next day being Thursday, we went again to the sessions at St. Margaret's Hill, where, about two in the afternoon, I was called to the bar. About an hour after I was called again and bidden to hold up my hand, which I did. My indictment was read, and it was a sharp one. Then my lord bade

me speak, and I answered briefly in this manner:

'Firstly, whereas I am charged in my indictment that I was reconciled – it is very true; to God almighty I so was, and I think lawfully might be. And, as I

continues on page 58

remember, it is allowed in your Book of Common Prayer, in the Visitation of the Sick, that if any man find himself burdened in conscience he should make his confession to the minister, which confession manifesteth a breach between God and his soul, and by this humble confession he craveth pardon of his sins and reconciliation to God again by the hands of his minister.

'Secondly, whereas I am charged that I was reconciled from my obedience to her Majesty and to the Romish religion, I will depose the contrary; for I was never reconciled from any obedience to my princess, for I obey her still, nor to any religion; for although I sometimes went to church against my will, yet was I never of any religion than the Catholic, and therefore needed no reconciliation to religion.

'Then', said the judge to the jury, 'you must consider of it. You see what is said; you cannot but find it treason by the law.'

"And so they went forth, and stood not long to think upon the matter, but came again, and I was called and bidden again hold up my hand. They bade the jury look on the prisoner, whether he is guilty or no: 'And who shall speak for you?'

"They all said, 'The foreman.'

"He spoke so softly I could not hear him. I willed him to speak up and not be afraid. Then he said, 'Guilty', to which I said with a loud voice, 'Laus tibi, Domine! Rex aterna Gloria.' When the rest were arraigned, and judgment was to be given, I was first called, and Justice Gaudy said, 'What canst thou say for thyself wherefore thou shouldst not

> "Bear witness with me, all good people, that I am now forthwith to give my life only for the Catholic cause."

'Thirdly, whereas in my former answers I said I went to church, it is true; for fear of temporal punishment I so did, but never minded to fall from the old religion, and therefore needed no reconciliation to religion.

'Fourthly, and lastly, I humbly beseech your good lordships, as you will answer it before God, to explicate the meaning of the statute to the jury. If the meaning thereof be to make it treason for a man fallen into the displeasure of God, through his sins, to be reconciled to God again, by him to whom God hath committed the authority of reconciliation; if this be treason, God's will be done.'

"Then said both the judges, 'It was by a Romish priest, and therefore treason.' I answered, 'It was by a Catholic priest, who had the liberty of the prison, and was free for any man to come to him to relieve him, and therefore by the statute no treason. Again, my lords, if it be not inquired of within a year and a day, there can be no advantage taken against me by this statute if you wrong me not.'

"Whereto replied one that sat under the judge, 'All this will not serve thy term, for the jury must find it treason.'

'Nay, then, sir,' said I, 'if it must be, let it be; God's will be done.'

"Then said Justice Gaudy, 'Her Majesty and her laws are merciful. If you will yet conform, and say here, before the jury going forth, that you will go to church, we will proceed no further.'

'My lord,' said I, 'if that be all the offence I have committed, as I know it is, and if there be no other way but going to church to help it, I would not wish your lordship to think I have, as I hope, risen thus many steps towards heaven, and now will wilfully let my foot slip and fall into the bottomless pit of hell. I hope in Jesus He will strengthen me rather to suffer a thousand deaths, if I had so many lives to lose. Let your law proceed.'

have judgment of death?'

"I answered, 'If that which before I have said will not serve, I can say no more.'

'Good Rigby,' said he, 'think not I seek your death. Will you yet go to church?'

'No, my lord.'

'Why, then,' said he, 'judgment must pass.'

'With a good will, my lord,' said I.

"Then he pronounced sentence, as you know the manner is, which, when he had ended, I said: 'Deo gratias; all is but one death, and a fleabite in comparison of that which it pleased my sweet Saviour Jesus to suffer for my salvation. I humbly thank your lordship for your great pains, and I freely forgive your lordship and the poor jury, and all other persecutors whatsoever.'

'Well said,' saith he. 'Indeed, you show your charity.' And then he gave judgment to the rest; and when he had done he called us together, willing us to send for a minister and provide for death. I desired his lordship to spare my presence, and bestow that counsel elsewhere, for I hope I am as well provided as by his exhortation as I should be.

'If you be,' said he, 'it is the better for you. God speed you well!'

"And so we parted. I pray God forgive them all, and amend them, if it be His holy will. Amen."

However, Judge Gaudy granted John a reprieve until he was brought before the next assizes on Thursday, 19th June, 1600, where Judge Kingsmel was sitting on criminal matters. Once again refusing to attend a Protestant service, the judge declared, "Then thou must die, for longer reprieve thou canst not have."

John replied, "My lord, that is the thing which I desire and look for, but I think myself far unworthy to die for so good a cause."

Seeing that John's legs were not restrained, the judge ordered that they be shackled. When the guard brought the chains, John took them in his hands, knelt down, making the Sign of the Cross before kissing his shackles.

The following day, John was again brought before the assizes. After much disagreement, Judge Kingsmel won through over Judge Gaudy and John was sentenced to death. John was returned to his prison cell and spent the rest of his time preparing himself through prayer.

The following morning (Saturday, 21st June), he was informed that he was to die that day, and received the news graciously. The minister from St. George's Church then came to visit him, hoping to help him in spiritual matters, but John declined his offer: "We two, sir, are opposite in religion, and therefore I must not communicate with you in matters of faith. I have long looked for death. I am prepared, fully resolved, and most ready to offer up my life for so worthy a cause. Fare you well, sir; I pray God make you a good man."

He was called for between five and six in the afternoon. Bidding farewell to his fellow Catholic prisoners, asking them for their prayers, he went down to the yard, knelt beside the waiting hurdle and made the Sign of the Cross. Beginning to pray, he was interrupted by the Under-Sheriff's deputy, Mr. More. Standing, John crossed himself and smiling, calmly lay on the vessel that would take him to his death, prompting people to wonder aloud if he was laughing out of happiness.

"Yes, verily, from my heart; and bear witness with me, all good people, that I am now forthwith to give my life only for the Catholic cause."

The deputy sternly responded, "You die for treason, for being reconciled by a seminary priest."

"Sir, I am a bachelor, and more than that, I am a maid."

"That is much," replied the Captain, "for a man of your years; you must have strove against your own flesh."

John replied, "I would be loath to speak anything contrary to the truth. I am indeed a maid and that is more than I needed to say."

"Then I see thou hast worthily deserved a virgin's crown. I pray God send thee the kingdom of heaven; I desire thee pray for me," concluded the Captain, full of admiration.

Reaching the place of execution, John was taken off the hurdle and led to the cart under the gallows, where he knelt down and prayed aloud until he was interrupted by the crowd for praying for the intercession of the saints. Helped up into the cart, he gave his executioner an angel of gold as a sign of forgiveness.

Turning to the crowd, he made the Sign of the Cross before praying for a few moments in silence. He kissed the noose as it was placed around his neck and then began to speak to the people before being halted by Mr. More (the same Sheriff's deputy mentioned before), who demanded he pray for the queen. John did this happily before the deputy asked him the names of any other traitors he knew in England. John replied that he knew none, causing the deputy to cry out in anger, "What?! If he will confess nothing drive away the cart!"

This order was done with such speed that John did not have enough time to commend his soul to God again, instead violently jerking as the rope around his neck halted his fall.

Shortly after, the deputy ordered the hangman to cut him down. This order was given so quickly that John was able to stagger on his feet, not being close to death at all. However, the executioners seized him and flung him to

"Yes, sir, but neither can that be treason, nor yet do I die for that only, for, as you know, the judge oftentimes offered to save my life if I would go to church," said John before pulling his hat down over his eyes and concluding, "In the name of Our Lord go on."

On his way to the place of execution – St. Thomas' Watering (now the Old Kent Road) – he was met by the Earl of Rutland and Captain Whitlock, who demanded to know his details and why he was to die. After urging John to conform, Captain Whitlock asked the condemned man if he was married.

the ground but John said loud and distinctly, "God forgive you. Jesus receive my soul." John's voice was cut out by a nearby porter – not even an executioner – putting his foot across John's throat, making it difficult for him to breathe.

Others held his arms whilst the executioner began to disembowel and dismember him. Still alive as they began to tug at his heart, John's body twisted in pain, throwing off those who were pinning him down.

Finally, they cut off his head and quartered him, disposing of his head and body parts around Southwark.

# Anne Line, laywoman, Tyburn, 1601

Anne Line was born c. 1568 in Great Dunmow, Essex. Her father was William Heigham, a fervent Calvinist, who was enraged when his daughter, Anne, and her brother, William, converted to Catholicism and so disowned and disinherited them. Shortly after converting, Anne married another convert, Roger Line, in the early 1580s, whilst both were still teenagers. The newly-weds pledged to help the Church in any way they could, moving to a house just outside Bishopsgate in London for the express purpose of helping and hiding priests.

However, during a Mass in 1585, both Anne's husband and brother were arrested and imprisoned. Roger, still only 19 years-old, was banished and lived until 1594 in the Low Countries. He never saw his wife again.

To confound the sense of loss, Anne was not a well woman. A widow to all extents and purposes, she continually suffered from headaches and oedema. Her body was so weak that every spring and autumn, her friends thought she was going to die. However, her soul was strong and vigorous, and she was a devout Catholic convert. She received the Blessed Sacrament at least once a week, always with tears in her eyes. Her usual topic of conversation was spiritual and she rarely discussed worldly vanities. More amazing was her desire to be a martyr - she even envied priests and others who seemed to be in a more advantageous position than her, or any of her gender, for receiving such a death!

However, she told her confessor some years before her death that William Thompson (sometimes Blackburn), a former confessor of hers who was martyred in 1586, had promised her that if God should deem him worthy of such an end, then he would pray that she too could receive the same happiness. Moreover, she related to her confessor a vision that she had received. Seeing Jesus bearing his Cross in the Blessed Sacrament, she had been invited to follow Him, indicating that she would receive the martyrdom she so desired.

Shortly after Roger's exile order, Anne became maid of honour to Penelope Rich, Countess of Warwick, a cousin of Queen Elizabeth, who lived at Leez Priory, not too far from Dunmow. However, she soon decided that this life was not her true calling.

When Fr. John Gerard established a refuge house for priests in London, it was given to Anne Line's charge. The threat of discovery constantly hung over her, meaning she was regularly having to find new lodgings, particularly after Fr. John Gerard's escape from the Tower of London in 1597, when the authorities suspected her of playing a role in his break-out. In the last eight years of her life she was running three adjacent refuge houses in London which quickly became a rallying point for local Catholics. One was her own house, in which she taught a number of young children; there was a retreat house for priests; and there was a detached abode for the resident chaplain.

Believing they had evidence that she was hiding a priest, the authorities beset her house at the very time Mass was being said on Candlemas Day (2nd February) 1601. However, the door stood firm and was strongly bolted, allowing the Jesuit priest - Fr. Francis Page - just enough time to change out of his vestments and escape. Eventually smashing their way in, the guards searched for anything in the house linked to Catholicism. No priest could be found but still they arrested Anne, along with Mrs. Gage, daughter of Baron Copley, who was found in the house at the time. After the intervention of a nobleman, Mrs. Gage was set free, but Anne was brought to trial at the Old Bailey before Lord Chief-Justice Popham, a bitter enemy of Catholicism, on 26th February.

As she was too weak and sick to walk after being held in the shocking conditions which were omnipresent in Elizabethan prisons, Anne had to be carried to the court in a chair. The evidence against her was very dubious; merely a testimony by a character named Marriot, who claimed that he had seen a man in Anne's house dressed in white, whom he presumed was a priest. With Mr. Popham's hatred, even this evidence was deemed sufficient for him to advise the jury to find Anne guilty of harbouring a seminary priest. The verdict returned, Popham sentenced Anne Line to death. She was sent back to Newgate prison to prepare herself for execution.

Whilst at Newgate, Anne revealed that she had received another vision the day before her condemnation. When reading her hours in her primer, Anne had perceived brightness upon and around her book, which she interpreted to be a sign of her future triumph. However, she resolved not to mention it till after her trial just in case, in his spitefulness, Popham had decided not to sentence her to death so that he could prove her vision to be a lie.

Anne showed no fear or change in her character when the keeper showed her the signed death warrant and she was carried off to her execution. At Tyburn, just before she was to die, she declared in a loud voice to the gathered crowd that had braved the stabbing cold and falling snow:

"I am sentenced to death for harbouring a Catholic priest, and so far I am from repenting for having so done, that I wish, with all my soul that where I have entertained one, I could have entertained a thousand."

Kissing the gallows and making the Sign of the Cross, Anne was suddenly left choking on the end of the rope as the cart was drawn away. After a brief struggle, she died.

Anne was executed before two condemned priests,

> *"I am sentenced to death for harbouring a Catholic priest, and so far I am from repenting for having so done, that I wish, with all my soul that where I have entertained one, I could have entertained a thousand."*

Roger Filcock and Mark Barkworth. The latter, who was next to die, embraced her dead body while it was still hanging, saying, "O blessed Mrs. Line, who hast now happily received thy reward! Thou art gone before us, but we shall quickly follow thee to bliss, if it please the Almighty."

Once it was dark, the staunchly Catholic Countess of Arundel sent men to gather Anne's remains, which had been thrown in a pit near the gibbet, which also contained the remains of wicked criminals who had suffered the same fate. The remains were taken from Tyburn to the Countess' house to be given a proper burial but the exact location is unknown.

*Anne Line suffered at Tyburn on 27th February, 1601.*

# Nicholas Owen, Jesuit laybrother, London, 1606

No details of Nicholas Owen's birth exist, neither details of his parents nor even where he was born, although it is believed to be around 1550 in Oxford. However, it would seem that he was born into a staunchly Catholic family as two of his brothers (John and Walter) became Jesuit priests and a third, Henry Owen, ran a Catholic printing press, which he managed to continue whilst in prison for recusancy. Probably a builder or carpenter by trade, Nicholas was consecrated by Fr. Henry Garnet (Superior of the English Jesuits), becoming one of the first Jesuit laybrothers some time before 1580. He took his skills with him, becoming a master priest hole builder. Despite being very small – his being just over five feet tall earned him the nickname 'Little John' – he was deceptively strong but, more importantly, very quiet. Always working alone at night, it was necessary for him to remain silent so that he did not disturb anyone in the house – servants could always report their masters to the authorities. Thus, he worked silently at night, digging into stonework, cutting through planking, whilst during the day he did carpentry work so that no one suspected his true purpose for being at the house. For example, at Braddocks (also known as Broadoaks) in Essex, he broke up and scooped out 80 cubic feet of masonry, apparently not once disturbing anyone in the house.

Furthermore, each hiding place had to be different; if a set plan was used all the time, one discovery by the pursuivants would have led to them always knowing where to look for the hiding places. Nicholas' constructions had to be extremely sophisticated. When searching for priests, the pursuivants would tap on all the walls of the house, listening for a hollow sound that would betray a hidden space, keeping an eye out for any uneven surface that could indicate secret building work. Thus, Nicholas employed various forms and methods, such as at Baddesley Clinton mansion near Warwick, where secret trapdoors in a priest hole beneath a window seat connected to the mansion's sewer system. Here, during a 1591 search, several priests hid in the sewers up to their waists in water for four hours. Elsewhere, he added 'feeding tubes' so that supplies could be passed down to the priests, who would sometimes have to hide for days at a time. Sometimes, this master craftsman even built 'fake' holes that could easily be discovered. These outer hiding places would actually contain an inner place but the pursuivants would be so busy watching the fake one that they wouldn't bother searching for another.

Nicholas created many priest holes but the exact number is unknown. Moreover, the tally keeps rising as they were so well hidden that they are still being discovered, often only when demolition or extensive rebuilding is being undertaken, proof of the incredible work performed by this little man. He would never accept payment for

his work and always received Communion and spent time in prayer before starting a job. Travelling the country, it was necessary for him to work under several aliases, including his nickname, Little Michael, Draper and Andrews.

Soon after Edmund Campion's execution in 1581, Nicholas was arrested after loudly proclaiming the martyr's innocence; he had been the priest's servant. After his release, he served both Fr. Henry Garnet and Fr. John Gerard for 18 years as their servant, journeying with them throughout England. He was captured with the latter in 1594 and the pair were viciously tortured on the 'Topcliffe rack', hanging for three hours from iron rings, with heavy weights on his feet pulling him down, agonizingly stretching his body to the point of tearing. However, Nicholas withstood the intense pain, refusing to give the authorities any information, and was released after a wealthy Catholic, knowing how vital the little man was to the safety of priests, bribed his jailors, who thought he was merely an insignificant acquaintance of John Gerard's.

However, this still left John Gerard imprisoned and it was Nicholas who was the mastermind behind the priest's fabled escape from the Tower of London in 1597. One night, one of Nicholas' conspirators – he was too well known himself – threw a length of string from Tower Wharf into the Cradle Tower. A rope was then drawn across the moat with the aid of the string, allowing John to make his escape back across the divide despite the great difficulty he had because his hands were virtually crippled by the tortures that had been inflicted upon him. Nicholas was waiting nearby with the horses to make good their escape.

During the severe repressions that followed the failed Gunpowder Plot, Nicholas was discovered at Hindlip Hall in Worcestershire, home of Thomas Abingdon, in early 1606. Having to utilise his own work, Nicholas and a companion hid in one of the 11 holes in the Hall for at least a week whilst 100 men tore the building apart in their search. Hidden in the house at this time were Nicholas, Fr. Henry Garnet, and another Jesuit and his servant, Fr. Edward Oldcorne and the Jesuit laybrother Ralph Ashley. Mixed with the terror that he would have no doubt been experiencing, hunger and starvation began to set in – the two concealed Catholics had retreated to their hiding place with only one apple between them after ensuring the priests were safely hidden with adequate provisions. After over a week, the pair were faint with hunger and in the end staggered from their hiding place and attempted

*Priests hiding places in Harvington Hall, some of them likely to be the work of Nicholas Owen. Harvington Hall, Kidderminster, Worcestershire DY10 4LR. Tel: 01562 777846.*

to escape. However, Nicholas was captured and immediately claimed to be Fr. Henry Garnet. He knew that claiming to be a priest would condemn him to death but he hoped that it would throw the pursuivants off the scent of the other priests who were still holed up elsewhere in the building. As it happened, the two priests succeeded in hiding for another week as they had much better supplies. They eventually crawled out from hiding doubled-up with cramp, only to be immediately arrested.

The authorities quickly learnt of Nicholas' true identity and were overjoyed. For example, the infamous Secretary of State, Cecil wrote, "It is incredible how great was the joy caused by his arrest … knowing the great skill of Owen in constructing hiding places, and the innumerable qualities of dark holes which he had schemed for hiding priests all through England." The Keeper of the Tower, Wade, was also made well aware of Nicholas' importance. After the craftsman was moved from his initial place of incarceration (Marshelsea) – where he had been allowed visitors in the forlorn hope that some priests would visit him, thus giving their identities away; Nicholas knew what was happening so spent his time in solitary prayer - to the Tower, the terrible 'examinations' began.

The rules were thrown out of the window in an effort to force Nicholas to reveal information, especially where he had built all his hiding places. English law forbade torturing anyone to death so, for this reason, also forbade torturing anyone who was already maimed in case their weaker state meant they unexpectedly died. Since 1599, Nicholas had walked with a pronounced limp after a packhorse fell on him and broke his leg. Thus, he should not even have been eligible for torture. This didn't stop the authorities though, who racked him day after day for excruciating six-hour sessions at a time. Furthermore, knowing that he suffered from a painful hernia, they viciously and spitefully wrapped an iron band around his middle, which they tightened to put further pressure on his hernia. The iron band also effectively held his stomach together, preventing it from being ripped apart during the merciless horrors through which he was put.

Nicholas was resilient though and would not say a word, revealing nothing about his constructions. Instead, he constantly called on Jesus and Mary to help him stand firm against the intense physical pain through which he was being put. In the end, his persecutors went too far and Nicholas died under the torture, the metal band failing in its job as his hernia ruptured and his stomach ripped apart, leaving his intestines to gush out onto the floor. Knowing that they had gone too far even for the times, the authorities attempted to claim that the Jesuit laybrother had committed suicide on 2nd March, 1606. However, Fr. John Gerard's famous narrative disproves this and a letter of Fr. Henry Garnet's shows Nicholas was still alive on 3rd March. Some even claimed that Nicholas Owen continued to suffer till as late as 12th November, a remarkable length of time to withstand such pain and continue to resist the temptation to halt the agony by revealing even just the smallest of details.

# Thomas Garnet SJ, Tyburn, 1608

Thomas Garnet was the son of Richard Garnet, a constant witness to, and sufferer for, the Catholic Faith and a fellow of Balliol College, Oxford. As such, whilst still a schoolboy at Horsham Grammar School, Sussex, before spending some time as page to Philip Howard, Earl of Arundel, Thomas spent a term in prison with the rest of his family for recusancy. He was also the nephew of Fr. Henry Garnet, who suffered in St. Paul's churchyard on 3rd May, 1606. From the day he was born in Southwark, Thomas' father had dedicated his son to God, so after initially educating him at home, he sent him abroad when he was 16 or 17 (1592) to the college at St. Omer. After completing his study of the humanities, Thomas crossed into the English College of Valladolid in 1595, where he was later ordained in 1599.

That same year, he was sent on the Mission with Mark Barkworth and laboured in England (predominantly round Warwickshire) with great zeal for six years, being noted for the number of converts he gained. Having desired to join the Jesuits for a long time, he was finally admitted into the Society by his uncle, Henry Garnet, who was the superior of the English Jesuits at the time. However, before he had a chance to cross to Europe to begin his novitiate, he was captured in 1605 near Warwick. Giving the name of Thomas Rookwood, probably after Ambrose Rookwood, who had been implicated in the Gunpowder Plot and at whose house (Coldham Hall) Thomas was acting as chaplain at the time, the captured priest was first sent to the Gatehouse gaol in Westminster before being committed to the Tower of London. As he was related to Henry Garnet and had recently received a letter from him, Cecil interrogated him at length, especially about the Gunpowder Plot, which had only recently been discovered. Despite threatening him with the rack, the authorities could find no evidence that he was involved in the plot. Instead, they kept him imprisoned for eight to nine months in a cell with no bed over a particularly harsh winter, leading to him developing rheumatic pains and a form of sciatica that persisted for the rest of his life.

Catholics did take it, then it was only through fear, to which he hoped he would not succumb.

He was sent to Newgate prison before standing trial at the Old Bailey upon an indictment of high treason for having been made a priest by authority derived from Rome and afterwards remaining in England. Three witnesses were brought forward who claimed that whilst Thomas was imprisoned in the Tower, he had scrawled in several places 'Thomas Garnet, priest'. The jury somehow found him guilty on this slender evidence and he was sentenced to death. Despite his friends offering him opportunities to escape the condemned cell that he was sent to, he always refused, hearing a voice from within that urged *Noli fugere* ("Don't run away").

When the time came, he approached his hurdle with great courage and even a certain cheerfulness in the knowledge that he was soon to win the martyr's crown. Thus, he laid himself upon the hurdle in a manner more appropriate to heading for a wedding feast rather than the cruel ignominious death of a criminal. Many people thronged the place of execution (an estimated crowd of a thousand), including a number of the nobility, such as the Earl of Exeter. The earl, a member of the Privy Council and Cecil's older brother, repeatedly urged the priest for over half and hour to save his life by taking the oath, claiming that several other Catholic priests had taken it and it was not a matter that concerned faith anyway. Therefore, Thomas should take the oath and embrace the king's offer of a reprieve by conforming just as others had done. Thomas steadfastly replied:

> ## "I will not take the oath, though I might have a thousand lives."

In 1606, Thomas was banished with 46 other priests, and headed to Louvain, where the English Jesuits had recently established a novitiate. He remained there for several months, encouraging the trainees, before returning to England in September 1607. However, he fell into the hands of the authorities six weeks later, this time betrayed by an apostate priest called Rouse. He was subsequently interrogated by Thomas Ravis, the Bishop of London, and Sir William Wade, superintendent of the keep and a notoriously cruel torturer of priests. Thomas refused to confirm or deny that he was a priest but steadfastly refused to take the new Oath of Allegiance, adding that if any

"My lord, if the case be so doubtful and disputable, how can I in conscience swear to what is doubtful as if it were certain? No, I will not take the oath, though I might have a thousand lives."

Disgruntled, the authorities ordered the priest into the cart. Cheerfully, Thomas complied, kissing the gallows that was to end his life and send him to heaven. He then professed that he was a priest and a Jesuit, although unworthy of such honours. He said that he did not admit this at his trial not through fear or shame, but because he did not want to be his own accuser and force the judges to condemn him to death. He admitted that he had spent nine years assisting and comforting the persecuted Catholic population, and converting many Protestants, but never had he ever dreamt of committing treason against the king. This prompted a minister to question whether his words were a little ambiguous, as to be a priest was to plot treason in their minds.

"No, sir," replied Thomas forcefully. "For if I had been minded to use equivocations, I might have taken the oath and saved my life; which oath I did not decline out of any unwillingness to profess my allegiance to the king, which I offered to do, and for that end produced at my trial a form of an oath of allegiance drawn up according to what was looked upon as satisfactory in the days of our forefathers, to which I was willing to swear. But this new oath is so worded as to contain things quite foreign to allegiance, to which in my opinion no Catholic can with a safe conscience swear."

Finally, the Earl of Exeter called out, "Did you write it?"

referring to the 'graffiti' that had condemned Thomas. "I did, my Lord," came the simple admission.

With that, Thomas crossed his hands before his breast and looked up to heaven, stating that this was the happiest day of his life. He was happy that he should die for this cause and prayed that God would not punish England for his death and to forgive all those who conspired against him, hoping that one day he might see them in heaven. Thomas then recited the Lord's Prayer, the Hail Mary, and the Creed and had just started the hymn *Veni Creator*, when the cart was pulled away at the line "*sermone ditans guttura*". He was left hanging until he died, as the crowd, especially the Earl of Exeter, would not allow the rope to be cut whilst he was still alive.

*Thomas Garnet suffered at Tyburn on 23rd June, 1608, aged 34. His relics were preserved at St. Omer but lost during the French Revolution.*

*They remember Catholic martyrs: marching from Newgate to Tyburn on the Annual Tyburn Walk in April 1961. Sadly, this popular public gesture of Catholic solidarity had to be abandoned following complaints from the Metropolitan police that the march caused too much traffic congestion!*

# John Roberts OSB, Tyburn, 1610

John Roberts was born at Trawsfynydd in Merionethshire, Wales, hence his being known as Father John de Menevia during his priesthood. He was the first prior of St. Gregory's, Douai, which is now known as Downside Abbey. Initially, he was at St. John's College, Oxford but left after two years (1597) to become a law student at one of the Inns of Court. In 1598, he travelled to the continent and was converted by a fellow countryman in Paris. Travelling to Spain, he entered the English College at Valladolid on 18th October, 1598. However, John felt called to the monastic life, which led him to enrol at the Benedictine abbey of St. Martin at Santiago de Compostela, making his profession on 6th April, 1600. Shortly after being ordained at Salamanca in 1602, he was sent on the English Mission on 26th December of the same year, apparently the first man from a monastery to enter England since the Reformation when he arrived in April 1603.

A man of great zeal, courage and steadfast faithfulness, he laboured for ten years on the Mission, being arrested and imprisoned on five separate occasions. Moreover, after each internment, he was banished but always returned with renewed vigour. During the great plague, which claimed 30,000 lives in London, John assisted many of the infected after hurrying back from his first exile, at the same time converting many of them by his example. During a 14-month exile after being banished in July 1606, John spent much of his time at Douai, founding a house for English Benedictine monks who had entered various Spanish monasteries. This was the beginning of the monastery of St. Gregory at Douai, which still exists today as Downside Abbey, near Bath. In total, John was exiled three times and escaped from prison on another occasion, reportedly filing through the bars of his cell window.

However, back in England, he was apprehended for the fifth and final time on the first Sunday of Advent (2nd December), 1610. Pounced upon whilst saying Mass, he was taken in his vestments and thrust into a dark dungeon. Not long after, he was brought to trial (5th December) and condemned to death for being a priest. He was offered a reprieve on condition that he took the Oath of Allegiance but he constantly refused.

On the day of his execution, he was dragged with Fr. Thomas Somers of Douai College to within 18 yards of the place of execution - Tyburn. The authorities had to stop sooner than planned because the throng of gentry and other people was so great that they could not reach the designated spot. Thus, the two priests had to be taken from their hurdle to the cart, where 16 other condemned prisoners waited with the ropes about their necks.

John was the first of the two to be ushered to the cart. With an air of cheerfulness he walked towards the place of death, still wearing his habit, and attempted to climb into the cart. However, he was too weak from a sickness, presumably contracted in the dungeon, and could not manage the small climb until the sergeant and other officers helped him up. He mentioned that he was to be hanged amongst common thieves, prompting one of the attending officers to proclaim that it was how Jesus had died.

As soon as he was up in the cart, John turned to the other sentenced men and lifted his hands to bless them, saying:

"We are all come hither to die, from which there is no hope of escape, and if you die in the religion now professed in England, you shall undoubtedly perish everlastingly: let me, therefore, for the love of our blessed Saviour, entreat you that we may all die in one faith, in testimony whereof let me beseech you to pronounce with me those words - I believe the holy Catholic Church. Protesting your desires to die members of the

*Statue of St. John Roberts, Downside.*

same, as also your sorrowfulness for having led so naughty and wicked lives, whereby you have offended our sweet and merciful Saviour; which if you will truly and constantly profess, I will pronounce absolution, and then my soul for yours."

Continuing with such counselling, a churlish officer interrupted him, forbidding him to speak any further to the prisoners. Upon this, John fell to his knees and prayed. Finishing, he stood and turned to face the crowd before openly blessing them all. The executioner then began removing John's habit whilst he requested permission to speak to the crowd. Being a man of renowned humility, the sheriff granted the priest's request, as well as having some water brought for him to prevent him from fainting because of his weakness.

Before he addressed the crowd, John helped his associate Fr. Somers up into the cart. After greeting him ("Welcome, good brother"), they embraced and blessed each other. John then turned back to the crowd, blessed them again and loudly started.

"*Audite coeli qua loquor, audiat terra verba oris mei.*" ("Honourable, worshipful, and my well beloved friends.")

No sooner had he started than the same loutish officer again interrupted him. So insolent was the officer that the crowd began to jeer him, protesting against his rudeness. Unable to continue upon the scripture text he had just spoken, John once more blessed the people and started afresh.

"I am condemned to die for that being a priest I came into England, contrary to a statute made in the 27th year of the late queen's reign. Other matter was not objected against me at my arraignment."

To the charge that he had entered England without due authority, John said that he had been sent to the country by the same authority that St. Augustine, the apostle of England, had been sent, and that he died for preaching the same religion that St. Augustine had planted in England. Surveying the crowd, he greeted every person with benedictions who saluted him with raised hat or otherwise, before declaring, "*Memorare novissima tua. Omnes nos manifestare oportet ante tribunal Christii.*" ("Let every man remember his end. We must all appear before the judgment seat of Christ.") before continuing, "there to give account of our faith and works. They that have done well shall go to everlasting life; and they that have done evil into everlasting torments."

Once more, he blessed the people, praying that they forgive him for only giving a short speech because of his illness. His last farewell was spent urging them to return to the unity of the Catholic Church, before adding that he would pray for them during the short time he had left, but would soon be in an even better position to do so in death. Once more, he was interrupted by the same officer, who scolded him for urging the people in such a matter. The head officer answered the complaint by arguing that the priest said nothing against the king or state, so there was no reason to stop him. The rude officer continued unabated though, arguing that it was not right for the people to be tempted in this way. John responded this time:

"I say nothing against the king, he is a good king; I beseech God to bless him, his grave senate, the council, the honourable bench by whom I was condemned, together with all those that have been instruments of my death. Neither is it the king that causes us to die, he is a clement king; it is heresy, it is heresy that does this."

Seeing the fire being prepared to burn his bowels, he commented, "I perceive you prepare a hot breakfast for us." Having given his last benediction, he brought his hands up close to his eyes and prayed silently until Fr. Somers had been prepared for his fate. With his hands tied, Fr. Somers blessed the people with these words: "*Benedicat vos omnipotens et misericors Dominus, Pater at Filius et Spiritus Sanctus.*" He continued, claiming that he was condemned to die for a being a priest and refusing to take the oath that the authorities maintained was one of allegiance. Protesting that he had always been a true, loyal and faithful subject, he expostulated that he refused not the oath, for the king was owed allegiance, but that it mixed with religion, which is forbidden by the Pope, whose authority all should follow. Therefore, he urged them all to obey this supreme pastor of God's Church affirming, just as John had done before, that there was no salvation outside of this Church.

Informed that they were now to die, the pair embraced and blessed each other, giving their last benedictions with bound hands. Placing his handkerchief over his eyes, John declared, "*Omnes sancti, et sancta Dei intercedite pro me,*" whilst Fr. Somers announced, "*In manu tuas Domine commendo spiritum meum.*"

Both were allowed to hang until they were dead. They were then cut down, disembowelled, beheaded and quartered before their entrails were burned and their quarters buried in the same pit that had been prepared for the other 16 wretches.

Two nights later, one of John's brethren, along with some other Catholics, dug up the quarters of the two martyrs at midnight. However, as they were returning into the town at the break of day, they were spotted by one of the night watchmen. Hurrying to escape, one of the pious thieves dropped one of John's legs, which was retrieved by the watchman and handed to George Abbot, Bishop of London and later the Archbishop of Canterbury. He had been John's chief adversary, and had stood with undisguised hostility and vehemence against John at his trial. He ordered the body part to be buried at the Church of St. Saviour so that the Catholics could not get hold of it. The rest of the body was successfully carried to the English Benedictines at Douai, except for one arm, which was sent to the abbey of St. Martin at Compostela. However, the body part in France disappeared during the French Revolution but two fingers can still be found - one at Downside Abbey, the other at Erdington Abbey.

*John Roberts suffered at Tyburn on 10th December, 1610, at the age of 34.*

# John Almond, priest, Tyburn, 1612

John Almond, who also called himself Francis Lathome before the Bishop of London and often went under the alias of Molineux, was born around 1577 on the edge of the Lancashire town known as Allerton, near Liverpool. He went to school at Much-Woolton in Lancashire but soon afterwards travelled to Ireland with his family.

Leaving home when he was 15 or 16 years-old, John went to Rheims, from whence he headed to Rome (at the age of 20) to train for the priesthood. Ordained in 1598, John was chosen to give the 'Grand Act' – a public defence of theses which covered the whole course of theology and philosophy - at the end of term, earning congratulations from the presiding Cardinals Baronius and Tarugi, who were greatly impressed by his debating skills. These rhetorical skills would be much in evidence in his future as he left Rome and returned to England in 1602, this time on the Mission.

Little is known of his actions in England, bar that he was arrested in 1608 but appears to have been released or banished shortly afterwards. He also seems to have worked chiefly in London. However, a portrait of his character exists that describes him as a sincere and holy man, who was worthy of being seen as a learned man. Furthermore, he shunned sin, setting a good example to all, yet was also courageous, modest and full of understanding. He was of average height but quite lean – whether through natural build or strict fasting is unknown. He had a thin face with very dark brown hair, which was showing specks of white by the time of his death.

John was captured for a second time on 22nd March, 1612. Seven priests had already escaped from prison that year and this may account for the zeal with which his persecutors went after him, particularly when he was brought before Dr. John King, who had recently been appointed Bishop of London. He was questioned lengthily and indignantly by Bishop King but outwitted and infuriated the hapless bishop throughout, refusing to take the oath to the queen or recognise that it was a central tenet of Catholicism that the Pope could depose kings. So embarrassed was Dr. King that he later described John as "a proud, arrogant jack" in a vain attempt to hide his own inferiority.

After the examination, John was sent to Newgate prison for several months before being brought to trial on an indictment of high treason, for taking orders abroad by the authority of Rome, and remaining in the country contrary to statutes that forbade it. During his imprisonment, the Archbishop of Canterbury visited John, hoping to gain his 'scalp' by convincing him to conform. However, like Dr. King, he was all but tied up by John's arguments and subsequently labelled the Catholic priest as "one of the learnedness and insolentest of the Popish priests." Such incidents may have been glorious, but John also suffered whilst in prison, being forced to live on a diet of tainted water and stale, mouldy bread. At his trial John apparently displayed the same level of wit which had left the hapless bishop floundering. However, this did not stop him being judged guilty by the jury despite neither confessing nor denying that he was a priest nor, evidently, any proof being brought against him as being so.

John's day of execution was 5th December, 1612. He was brought from Newgate to Tyburn between seven and eight o'clock in the morning, smiling as he lay on the sledge which was dragging him to his death.

Arriving at the site, John rose, had his hands untied and immediately removed his hat, thanking God in a loud voice that He had judged him worthy to receive the glorious martyr's crown. He then turned to the sheriff asking what exactly he was supposed to do next. Informed that he was to get in the cart beneath the gallows, the priest struggled to do so, his legs being stiff and weak after being kept in an extremely cold cell for the previous ten days.

Once up, he cheerfully announced, "I am now, I thank God, up," before blessing himself and praying silently. After a period, he was granted permission to speak to the crowd, prompting him to kneel in the cart, declaring, "*Domine labia mea aperies, et os meum annuntiabit laudem tuam*."

Protesting that he would not offend anyone, he announced that he was a Catholic who was there to die for his religion and Christ's cause, who had shed His blood for his redemption. Furthermore, John added that if he had more lives to lose and more blood to bleed for God, then he would happily follow the same route. From the bottom of his heart, he acknowledged that King James I was the true and lawful king, and that he was a loyal and true subject who had never had a treasonous thought as God was his witness. Moreover, John claimed that if he had known of any plots against the king, then he would have done everything in his power to halt the conspiracy. Thus, he prayed that God protect the king and the royal family, once more acknowledging that the king had authority to make laws which his subjects were bound to obey.

However, he was here interrupted by a Protestant minister who demanded to know why he, a priest, broke those laws then by coming into the country. John calmly responded that Christ was the greater King and that laws made against His laws were not binding. Besides, John added, the authorities had not yet proved he was a priest and, if he was, he had a remit from Jesus to enter England anyway – "Go therefore and make disciples of all nations" (Matthew 28:19) – just as he assumed Protestants would enter the likes of Turkey to spread the Word, despite the threat of death.

Irate at John's response, the minister launched into a diatribe against him, accusing him of preaching dangerous doctrines at his trial, like that a priest could forgive and absolve a man who killed a king, and that he had treated the bench with rude contempt. Refusing to rise to the bait, John coolly answered that the minister had mis-represented Catholic doctrine and that the Faith viewed murder as a most heinous crime. Nor did it encourage any sin, let alone treason – rather, its doctrine taught humility, patience and obedience. However, no matter the evil of the sin or how wicked the sinner, if they truly repented and sought forgiveness, then thanks to Christ's Passion they could be forgiven.

John added that Christ Himself had said as much and granted that power to the Catholic Church; whichever sins they forgive are forgiven in heaven, and so on.

The minister, ignoring John's query of whether this was also Protestant doctrine or did they ignore the Bible, then demanded to know of John what possible penance could be made for the murder of a king. Despite John replying that Christ's death was satisfaction enough, the minister pressed him further but John kept to his argument, before asking to be left a minute for silent prayer.

others that way, whom God forgive, for I do. For I, having been a prisoner there since March, [can say that] we have been ill-treated continually, but now at last without charity; we were all put down into the hole or dungeon, or place of little ease, whence was removed since we came thither two or three cart loads of filth and dirt. We were kept 24 hours without bread or meat or drink, loaded with irons, lodging on the damp ground, and so continued for ten days or thereabouts."

The Sheriff stopped him here, telling him that the prison keeper had just been carrying out orders, prompting John to state, "I had thought it had been done of his own head; but since it was done by power, I will neither resist it, nor speak further of it."

Turning to the executioner, he handed him a gold coin worth 11 shillings, adding, "I don't give thee this to spare me, for I am ready, as my duty doth bind me, to lose both

> *"And yet not death, for death is the gate of life unto us, whereby we enter into everlasting blessedness; and life is death to those who do not provide for death, for they are tossed and troubled with vexations, miseries and wickedness. But to use well this life is the pathway, yet through death, to everlasting life."*

However, another minister interrupted, claiming that John's argument had disproved his protestations of loyalty. Tirelessly, John told him that this was not the case; the only reason he had refused to take the Oath of Allegiance, as they called it, was out of conscience due to the clauses that it held. If the Pope or any foreign ruler sought to invade England and depose the rightful ruler, then, said John, they should be resisted – this was what Catholic doctrine taught. The Faith was to be established not by blood and war but by the example of Christ and His apostles. It was this that he had always professed and he was ready to seal it with his blood.

John was then stripped down to his breeches and a waistcoat, but his halter left around his neck. The condemned priest knelt again and began to pray, thanking God for giving him the strength to die for the Catholic religion, whose every tenet he believed. Once more, a minister interrupted him, informing John that he had forgotten to pray for the forgiveness of his sins. John requested he stop interrupting, scolding him that he could not pray for everything at once, but was going to pray for that even without the minister's rude promptings.

Standing, John drew several objects from his pockets and gave them to members of the awaiting crowd. He also distributed three or four pounds worth of silver to the poor who were present and had crowded about the gallows, saying: "I have not much to bestow or give, for the keeper of Newgate hath been somewhat hard unto me and

life and blood," before continuing that there was no torture too severe, whether that be ripping him apart whilst still alive, or tearing each joint from the other. Instead, he just hoped that God would keep him strong and that the blood he was about to spill was not nearly the amount he was willing to expend for Christ.

Kneeling down again, he acknowledged that he was a sinner and begged for God's forgiveness, hoping that Christ, by His mercy and Passion, would pardon him, and that He would accept his willingness to shed his blood for His glory. Immediately, a minister called out, denouncing John: "What?! Do you match and compare, then, your blood-shedding with Christ's blood-shedding, as if Christ were not able to work your salvation without your own means?"

Once more, John did not take the bait: "You mistake me – my sins, though venial, deserve Christ's wrath and punishment. It is His death alone, and the shedding of His blood alone, that is not only sufficient but also efficient to save us all. I have not much more to say – one hour overtaketh another, and though never so long, at last cometh death. And yet not death, for death is the gate of life unto us, whereby we enter into everlasting blessedness; and life is death to those who do not provide for death, for they are tossed and troubled with vexations, miseries and wickedness. But to use well this life is the pathway, yet through death, to everlasting life."

*continues on page 70*

Now stripped down to just his shirt, John again knelt, repeating in Latin, "Into Thy hands, O Lord, I commend my spirit; Thou hast redeemed me, O Lord God of truth!" (*"In manus tuas Domine…"*). He then waited patiently, showing no sign of fear, while the executioner prepared for the imminent tortures. Smiling, John urged any Catholics present to pray for him, repeating the above prayer again. Further heartened, he swore that he died a virgin, detesting the carnal acts and sins with which people had attempted to slander the Church and its priests. Thanking God, he said, "I have been indicted and accused that I was a priest, but I will neither confess nor deny the same. But at the last day, when all secrets are revealed and Christ shall come in glory to judge the world – to whom I hope I am now going – He will then reveal what I am."

Ready to die, having stood for a lengthy period nearly naked in the freezing cold, he offered his hands to the executioner to tie them together. Ready for the cart to be pulled away, John asked if it was not the custom to have a handkerchief covering his eyes. The crowd responded positively and one of them tried to give him a filthy handkerchief as a final act of humiliation. However, this was refused and, at the last moment, a clean one was tied over his eyes.

Ready to die, John asked the executioner to let him know when the cart was to be pulled away so that he could die with the name of Jesus on his lips. He continued to repeat the prayer, "In manus tuas Domine…" and, the sign being given, cried out, "Jesu! Jesu! Jesu!" as the cart was pulled away and the rope went taught, snapping tight around his neck.

As he hang, choking slowly and agonisingly, several onlookers rushed forward, pulling on his legs to help him die before he would be cut down and forced to face the agony of the butchery that would come next. However, he was cut down whilst still alive and died as his body was being ripped apart.

*John Almond died at the age of 45, during his 11th year on the mission, at Tyburn on 5th December, 1612.*

An interesting appendix to the story of John Almond is provided by what happened after to Dr. King, Bishop of London, who had been such a stringent promoter of John's execution. After the death of the priest, Dr, King is said to have sunk in to a life of sorrow rather than being happy at bringing about the poor priest's death. Furthermore, Catholic writers of the time claim that this led to him becoming a Catholic and dying in communion with the Church that he had so viciously persecuted. In the preface of a book published in his name after his death, entitled *The Bishop of London's Legacy*, he addressed John: "O happy Almond, who here upon earth didst mask thyself under the name of Molineux! In thy blood did I wash my hands. It was I that did further thy death. Be thou, O blessed saint, who now seest and hearest me – *Quid non videt, qui videntem omnia videt?* What does he not see, who sees Him that sees all things? – be thou, I say, out of thy charity as propitious to pray for the remitting of that crying sin, as I am ready to acknowledge the sin. And let thy blood (guilty of no other treason than in not being a traitor to Christ and His Church) not resemble the blood of Abel, which cried for revenge against his brother, but rather the blood of Christ, which prayed for pardon of His crucifiers."

## RELICS
and links to the martyrs

St. Margaret Clitherow's right hand is preserved at the Bar Convent in York. Established in 1686, it is the oldest surviving convent in England.

Further information can be obtained from: The Bar Convent, 17 Blossom Street, York, North Yorkshire, YO24 1AQ. Tel: 01904 643238 Email:info@bar-convent.org.uk

www.bar-convent.co.uk

Museum and convent tours are available.

*(right)* St. Oswald's houses the Holy Hand of St. Edmund Arrowsmith, who was executed in Lancaster in 1628. The hand has been preserved ever since; it is said to possess miraculous powers and was approved for public veneration in 1934.

Further information: St. Oswald and St. Edmund Arrowsmith's Church, Liverpool Road, Ashton-in Makerfield, Wigan, Lancashire WN4 9NP. Tel: 01942 727249.

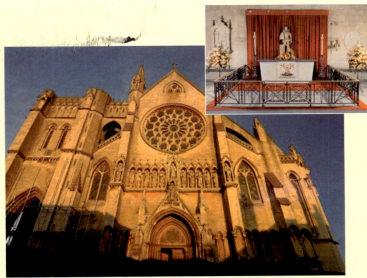

At the end of the north transept of Arundel Cathedral is the shrine of St. Philip Howard, Earl of Arundel, who died as a prisoner in the Tower of London in 1595.

The shrine to the saint has a fine statue of St. Philip in Elizabethan costume and contains his relics.

Further information:
Cathedral House, Parsons Hill, Arundel, West Sussex BN18 9AY. Telephone: 01903 882297.
www.arundelcathedral.org

Base of St. John Payne and containing several viewable priest holes as well as a mesmerising collection of items relating to Catholic history and the Catholic Petre family, 16th century Ingatestone Hall is only one mile off the A12.

Further information: Ingatestone Hall, Hall Lane, Ingatestone, Essex CM4 9NR. Tel: 01277 353010.

# Edmund Arrowsmith SJ, Lancaster, 1628

Born in 1585 at a place called Haydock in Lancashire, five miles from Warrington and seven from Wigan, Edmund Arrowsmith was the son of Robert, a farmer, and Margery. Both of his parents were devout Catholics and had suffered for their religion, just as their families had a record for doing. For example, Edmund's grandfather, Thurstan Arrowsmith, was jailed for a very lengthy period after having his assets taken away from him on account of his Catholicism; he died whilst in prison. His grandfather on his mother's side, Nicholas Gerard, had also never wavered in his Catholic faith. In fact, so well known was he for this that his own brother, Sir Thomas Gerard, ordered him to be forcibly carried to a Protestant service despite him being unable to move due to a vicious bout of gout. However, Nicholas refused to join in the service with the minister or congregation, instead singing psalms in Latin so loudly that he eventually had to be removed from the church because the minister could not be heard. Furthermore, Margery was a cousin of the famous Fr. John Gerard, one of the few prisoners to escape from the Tower of London.

Edmund's parents had been punished financially on several occasions and had even had their house searched by pursuivants. During the search, every bed was speared with a sword and several walls knocked through to ensure that no priest or any apparatus of the Mass was hidden anywhere. Despite checking every possible place in which any incriminating evidence could be hidden and finding nothing, the couple were tied together and driven to Lancaster prison. Shockingly, they were forced to leave behind their four children, including Edmund, who the pursuivants had driven from their beds in their nightshirts and left to stand in that way out in the freezing night. It was only when some neighbours saw the poor children that they were rescued from their ordeal.

Robert Arrowsmith, able to pay for his and his wife's release as he had done in the past, left the country to escape the persecutions, heading to Holland and serving in the wars there for a while, in which his brother, Peter, died. Robert then travelled to Douai College to see another brother, Fr. Edmund Arrowsmith, who taught in the college, before returning to England, where he died shortly after. This left Mrs. Arrowsmith as a widow with little money as she continued to be regularly fined for refusing to attend the compulsory Protestant services. In an effort to help her, a kindly priest took the young Edmund into his protection, hoping to ease her burden and to educate the youngster in Catholic teaching.

After finishing his schooling – all schooling was Protestant then – which had been corrected out of hours by the priest, Edmund attempted to travel to one of the Spanish seminaries but could not secure a safe passage. However, he had more success in reaching Flanders, where he entered the English College of Douai in December 1605.

Soon after his arrival, Edmund was confirmed. Previously, he was known as Brian but he took the name Edmund, after his uncle, as his confirmation name, being known as Edmund Arrowsmith from that day onwards. Completing his humanities studies, he had to return to England because of poor health but quickly returned, despite his health still being frail, to train as a priest. However, he worked so hard that his health again began to fail to such an extent that he twice received Extreme Unction because it seemed as if he would die. His superiors decided that as he was almost ready for ordination, he would be made a priest early and sent on the mission to England. Therefore, he received his lesser orders at St. Nicholas' Church in Douai on 14th June, 1612 and, later that same year, on 9th December, he was ordained as a Catholic priest in Arras. On 17th June, 1613, less than a year after his ordination, Dr. Kellison, who had recently been appointed as President of the College, sent him upon the English Mission.

Back in England, Edmund's health quickly recovered and he undertook his work with impressive zeal in his native Lancashire. Edmund was a man who had a great presence that at times seemed almost oppressive, with a facial expression that often looked less than inspiring. However, beneath this exterior, he was cheerful, witty and industrious. Furthermore, he was also ever eager to dispute with Protestants over theology, often risking alerting the authorities to his presence because of his vigour. One fellow priest noted that he often had to keep Edmund from taking on groups of Protestant ministers because it would have brought the whole weight of the community down upon them. The same priest also recounted how a Protestant gentleman had seen the company and discovered that Edmund was a priest. The gentleman, thinking that he would abuse and outwit the priest, began to taunt him but his jibes were thrown back with such ferocity by Edmund that the gentleman swore an oath, proclaiming, "I thought I had met with a silly fellow, but now I see he is either a foolish scholar or a learned fool."

Edmund was also noted for performing exorcisms, which he always undertook with several other priests rather than facing them alone. After working for ten or 11 years as a secular priest, Edmund became a Jesuit in 1624. Notably, he did not go abroad for his noviceship but travelled to Essex for a two or three month spiritual retreat.

Prior to his becoming a Jesuit, Edmund had been arrested in about 1622 and imprisoned in Lancaster. However, he was soon pardoned and released with several others but not before being brought in front of Dr. Bridgman, Bishop of Chester, and several other ministers who were all at dinner, eating meat despite it being Lent. For his part, Dr. Bridgeman explained that he was eating meat because of his age and infirmity, prompting Edmund to question, "But who dispenses with your lusty ministers there, for they have no such need?" Throughout the meal, the ministers argued with him, verbally attacking him continuously, resulting in Edmund chiding the bishop, "Turn all your dogs loose at once against me, and let us have a loose bait."

His final apprehension was just before the summer assizes in 1628. Edmund had attempted to advise a young man who had fallen far from God. He had also reproached the same individual for committing incest with his mother. The young man, full of hatred for this priest who had told him how wrong his actions were, told a Justice of the Peace, called Captain Rawsthorn, where to find him. Rawsthorn immediately issued a warrant for the priest's arrest and he was captured on Brindle Moor and taken to the Boar's Head Inn, before being brought to Lancaster Castle, where he was promptly thrown into prison for refusing to take the oath and on suspicion of being a Jesuit and a priest.

Sir Henry Yelverton was to sit at the assizes and had Edmund brought before him with other common criminals the following day – 26th August. Seeing Edmund's fierce looks, Judge Yelverton immediately sent for his colleague, Sir James Whitelock, sensing that Edmund could be troublesomely defiant. The jury set, Judge Yelverton asked Edmund if he was priest. Blessing himself with the Sign of the Cross, Edmund replied, "I would to God I were worthy." Judge Yelverton asked him the question again but received the same answer. Changing tack, he then asked, "Are you then no priest?" but Edmund simply remained silent.

Thus, the judge turned to the jury, telling them, "You may plainly see he is a priest? I warrant you he would not for all England deny his order." A minister then whispered to the judge and promptly began haranguing Edmund as a seducer who would make half of Lancashire papists if he were not stopped. In response, Edmund requested that the ban, which the judge had earlier announced, on him talking about his faith be lifted. The judge told him that the Catholic doctrine could not be maintained and argued for but said that Edmund could speak in defence of his religion so that other Catholics could hear its doctrine ripped to shreds, prompting Edmund to defiantly say that he would gladly defend it with more than words by happily sealing it with his blood. This riled the judge who started to abuse Edmund, telling him

that he would die and see his bowels burn before his face.

Calmly, Edmund responded, "And you, my Lord, must die too."

The judge was enraged, ordering Edmund to tell him how he could justify going abroad and training as a priest, thus breaking the law. Once more, Edmund remained cool: "If any man can lawfully accuse me, I stand ready here to answer him." However, there was no proof apart from one of the judge's servants swearing that Edmund had tried to convert him by claiming that Protestantism was a heresy which started with Luther, and the judge's 12 year-old son, who alleged that Edmund had attempted to convert him, although he would not claim this under oath.

Given permission to speak, Edmund stated:

"My Lords, as I was travelling in this country, that very man [the servant], as I take it, rushed forth upon me by a hillside with a drawn sword in his hand. His apparel was mean, but he was on horseback. I made as much haste from him as I could, but yet being a weak and sickly man, he forced me in the end to the moss, where I left my horse, and then I fled with all the speed I could use, but yet that could not be great in regard I was laden both with heavy clothes and books, and other things. At length, he came up to me at a moss ditch and struck at me, who had no other defence but a little walking stick, and a dagger which I drew not; and, as for the stick, he cut it close off at the hand by the blow he gave me and did me withal some little hurt. I asked him then what his meaning was and whether he intended to take my purse and my life. He answered that perhaps he would; and then I fled again from him, but he took me more quickly. And then came in this very youth [the judge's son] who hath offered to give evidence against me, and some others also to assist him. They used me very unworthily and carried me first to an alehouse and searched me to the very skin, after a barbarous manner, and offered some such other indignities as modesty forbids me to relate. But therein I hindered them the best I could, and that done they fell to drink; and so they consumed nine shillings of my money in one hour. And they told me

*continues on page 74*

the Justice himself, by whose warrant they had apprehended me, was there in person, but that I knew not how to believe. Upon these occasions, my Lords, I began to find fault with this man's wicked and rude behaviour, who seemed to be the ringleader of the rest, and I besought him for Jesus' sake to give over his disorderly life, his drinking, swearing, dissolute talking, and all those other things, whereby he might offend Almighty God. Upon my word, and upon my life, this, or to this effect is all that I said to him. Let him look on me and gainsay it if he can. As for that youth, I deny not to have told him that I hoped when he came to riper years, he would look better into himself, and become a true Catholic; for that, and that alone, would be the means to save his soul, to which he made no answer at all. And I hope, my Lords, that neither they nor any other can prove an ill thing against me."

Upon this, the judge began to inveigh against him bitterly, denouncing him as an evil seducer who should never be released to repeat his evils. Edmund fell to his knees in response and besought God to bless the King, the Privy Council and everyone there, and asked that God root out all heresy so that they could all be one religion again. Enraged, Judge Yelverton furiously roared, "Look you, gentlemen of the jury, how he wishes God to confound us all, and root out heresy, by which he means our religion."

Edmund was then sent to a deep dungeon in isolation whilst the judge drew up an indictment against him. Judge Yelverton quickly decided to charge him with being a priest and a Jesuit upon the testimony of the incestuous mother and son who had first contacted the Justice about the priest. He was also to be charged as a seducer in religion on the basis of the testimony heard in court. Thus, Edmund was brought back to the court, with Judge Yelverton this time sitting alone. The jury duly pronounced him guilty of high treason and the judge then asked Edmund why his life should be spared. Looking up to heaven and raising his hands in the same direction, Edmund made no sound, just awaited the inevitable.

The judge then announced that he was to die in the usual manner, commenting sadistically: "Know shortly thou shalt die aloft, between heaven and earth, as unworthy of either; and may thy soul go to hell with thy followers." Immediately, Edmund fell to his knees upon hearing the sentence, bowed his head and boomed "*Deo gratias*", before thanking God in English. The gaoler then led Edmund to prison and carried out the judge's command that he should be bound in the heaviest irons they could find. Once these were put upon him and he could barely move, Edmund recited the psalm *Miserere* in a loud voice. On reaching the prison, the wretched priest was thrown in what could best be described as a tiny, dark hole, in which he could not even lie down. Instead, he was forced to sit, cramped-up in the same clothes from one or two o'clock on Tuesday till midday Thursday, when he was fetched for execution. During this painful time, three or four of the Sheriff's men watched him continuously, just as the judge had commanded. Furthermore, the judge had also dictated that if any man spoke to him, they would be fined £100. It is believed that he was given nothing at all to eat or drink during this time.

Despite no one being allowed to talk to Edmund, the minister who had bitterly attacked him in court was given leave to do so, but only because he would argue with the poor priest about the validity of Catholic doctrine. However, Edmund refused to receive him, fearing what lies might be told about him after his death. Unfortunately, the minister and some of his followers decided that this meant Edmund was not very intelligent and scared to do 'verbal battle' with them because he knew he would lose.

Meanwhile, Edmund prepared himself for death and was informed on 28th August that he was to die within four hours, prompting him to proclaim, "I beseech my Redeemer to make me worthy of it!" The judge had decreed that he was to die at noon so that few people would witness the dubious sentence being carried out because they would be having their lunch. However, the number present to see him brought out and handed to the Sheriff for execution was astounding and far bigger than anyone could ever have imagined. This was replicated by the throngs that lined the streets as he was carried to his death.

As he was carried though the prison-yard, a fellow-prisoner, the condemned but later reprieved Fr. John Southworth (later martyred), appeared at the window of his cell. Edmund saw him there and raised his hands, and John promptly gave the sign which had been arranged to indicate the public absolution of Edmund's sins. As Edmund was being brought towards the gates, a Catholic gentleman jumped out and embraced him before being forcibly removed from the condemned priest's path. Lying down on the hurdle, Edmund was forced to have his head by the horse's back-end as a further act of humiliation. He was dragged a quarter of a mile through the streets to his place of execution in this position, all the while guards preventing anyone who may have offered him any consolation getting close-by. However, they did allow ministers to berate him, further heightening his torment. All the while, the executioner led the gruesome parade, menacingly beating a club into his hand. In stark contrast, Edmund clutched two papers – the dua claves coeli – one containing an act of love for God, the other an act of contrition.

Drawing towards the gallows, the cortege halted and the old minister named Mr. Lee, who had harangued him throughout and suffered from a limp, leered towards Edmund, gesturing at the huge fire over which there was a cauldron full of boiling, bubbling water: "Look what is provided for your death; will you conform yourself yet and enjoy the mercy of the king?" Edmund replied without a hint of anger in his voice, "Good sir, tempt me no more. The mercy which I look for is in heaven, through the death and Passion of my Saviour Jesus, and I most humbly beseech Him to make me worthy of this death."

He was then violently dragged from the hurdle to the ladder's foot, where they untied him. Edmund began to pray, repeating the words he had uttered regularly whilst on his way to the execution spot – "I freely offer Thee my death, O sweet Jesus, in satisfaction for my sins; and I wish this little blood of mine may be a sacrifice for them." The same minister then pounced on Edmund's words, accusing him, "You attribute nothing to Christ's merits and Passion," to which Edmund replied, "O sir, say not so – Christ's merits and Passion are always pre-supposed." He then prayed for 15 minutes before the sheriff told him that that was enough, ordering him to mount the ladder. "God's will be done," replied the condemned priest and, undaunted, he kissed the ladder before beginning the climb towards his death.

As he was climbing, Edmund requested that all Catholics present pray for him as he faced his final battle. Sneering, the minister taunted him, falsely claiming that there were no Catholics there but he would pray for him anyway. Defiantly, Edmund ceased his climb and turned towards the minister: "I neither desire your prayers, nor will pray with you; and if it be true what you say – that there are no Catholics here – I wish I might die as many deaths as there are people in this place, upon condition that they were all Catholics." He then requested forgiveness from any he might have offended, as well as forgiving those who had plotted his death.

Going a little higher, Edmund again stopped and, once more demonstrating his desire to debate, he turned to address the crowd: "You gentlemen, who are come hither to see my end, bear witness with me that I die a constant Roman Catholic and for Jesus Christ's sake. Let not my death be a hindrance to your well-doing and going forward in the Catholic religion, but rather an encouragement therein. For Jesus' sake have a care of your souls, than which nothing is more pre-cious. And become members of the true Church, as you tender your salvation, for hereafter that alone will do you good. I beseech you request my brethren, for His sake who redeemed us all, to be careful to supply my want and insufficiency, as I hope they will. Nothing doth so much grieve me as this England, which I pray God soon convert."

Pausing, Edmund silently said a final prayer before pulling his hat over his eyes, awaiting the inevitable push that would send him from the ladder. However, the taunting minister was not finished with him yet: "Sir, I pray you accept the king's mercy, conform yourself, and take the oath, and you shall live. Good sir, you shall live; I would fain have you live. Here is one now from the Judge to offer you mercy – you shall live if you will conform yourself to our religion."

Resisting the temptation placed before him, Edmund lifted the hat from his eyes, politely requesting: "O Sir, how far I am from that? Tempt me no more – I will not do it, in no case, on no condition." Edmund then bid the Sheriff and all present to take care of their souls, prompting some ministers to mutter aloud that they and the crowd were well capable of doing that without his wicked urgings. Others in the gathered mass began to turn angry and restless, shouting aloud, "No more of that, no more of that! Away with him, away with him!"

Resignedly, Edmund once again pulled the hat over his eyes. Beginning to pray loudly, he was promptly cast off the ladder at the will of the baying crowd, the words "*Bone Jesu*" (O good Jesus) the last to be heard from his mouth.

Left to hang until he had finally choked to death, Edmund's body was cut down, disembowelled and quartered. His head was then set upon a pole and placed at the top of Lancaster castle for all to see, whilst his four quarters were displayed prominently elsewhere around the same building.

Despite many who had seen the spectacle thinking the events barbaric and quite sickening, the following day, the judge spotted Edmund's head on the top of castle. Deciding it was not obvious enough, he ordered that it be raised another six yards in the air so that nobody could miss it. Unusually for a judge, Yelverton had watched the execution through his telescope before sitting down to dinner. As he finished his meal, portions of the dismembered body were brought from the scaffold cauldron and placed next to some newly-arrived venison, prompting the judge to crack a few coarse and inappropriate jokes. Eighteen months later, the wicked judge died, suffering a stroke that saw him exclaim in his agony, "That dog Arrowsmith has killed me."

That following day – 29th August – also saw the execution of a serious criminal whom Edmund had converted, Richard Hurst. The newly repentant Hurst died showing great signs of remorse for his crimes and standing firm in his new Catholic faith, refusing the offer of his life if he conformed back to Protestantism.

*Edmund Arrowsmith was martyred on 28th August, 1628, at the age of 43, during his 15th year on the mission, his fifth as a Jesuit. His hand is preserved as a relic at St. Oswald's Church in Ashton-in-Makerfield (see p71).*

*Lancaster Castle, Castle Parade, Lancaster LA1 1YJ.*
*Tel: 01524 64998*
*www.lancastercastle.com*

# Ambrose Barlow OSB, Lancaster, 1641

Edward Barlow was known as Fr. Ambrose during his priesthood. He was born at Barlow Hall near Manchester in 1585 to a very Catholic family. His father, Alexander Barlow, was the Knight of Barlow Hall. Edward was baptised at Didsbury Church on 30th November, 1585. His father ensured that he was given a Catholic education so the child's natural inclination to piety and learning was strengthened. At the age of 12, Ambrose was removed from his school and employed as page to a wealthy relation. However, as he grew up he began to consider the emptiness of this life in comparison to eternal life so decided to withdraw from this vacuous world by going abroad, becoming a priest and thus acquiring the means to help his native country.

As many learned priests had already come out of Douai, it was there that he decided to head. Meeting two others of a similar age and inclination, he roomed with them and completed his education at the Benedictine monastery of St. Gregory in Douai. Having finished his study in humanities, Ambrose headed to the English College at Valladolid on 23rd August, 1610, entering it on 20th September. Here, Ambrose undertook his philosophy course and some of his divinity. However, before he had finished the latter subject, he followed his brother, Dr. William Rudesind Barlow, back to Douai, where he entered the Benedictine Order. He completed his noviceship at a house then belonging to the English congregation near St. Malo in Little Brittany, being professed at Douai in 1616. Shortly after (1617), he was ordained and sent upon the English mission to which he found himself called.

His missionary labours were concentrated in Lancashire, where he converted large numbers through his preaching and example. He was so zealous that if he had not completed some act for the salvation of souls in a day then he viewed that day as one lost. No matter the hour of the night or day, he was ready to reclaim a lost soul and any time he did not use for devotions he spent hunting for those in need. He regularly celebrated Mass with great reverence. Moreover, he kept fixed hours for daily prayer that he never missed and recited the Rosary daily. He held especially dear the devotions to the Passion and Resurrection of Christ, as well as to Our Lady. Furthermore, he often meditated on Christ's sufferings, doing so whilst he held his arms extended as if on the Cross. In such a way, he began to desire to suffer for his Redeemer and prayed daily for this reward.

Ambrose bore a great contempt for the world and its vanities whilst holding himself in low esteem in comparison to the high opinion, love and veneration he had for the virtue of others. He was afraid of all honours and described vanity as the worm or moth of virtues. Any feasts or parties that may have led to excess and idle chat were avoided and he had no interest in secular issues. Despite their requests, he refused to live solely with the wealthy families of the area, preferring to live in a country house where the poor could call on him at any time. His main bases were Wardley Hall, situated just outside Manchester and seat of the Downe family (his skull is preserved there), and Morley's Hall in Leigh, seat of the Tyldesley family, seven miles from Manchester. Pastoral visits were always made on foot whilst he refused a servant until sickness forced otherwise. His clothes were always poor and he refused to wear a watch or carry a sword. Moreover, he boarded with an honest farmer, eating mostly white meats and vegetables, whilst drinking little beer and abstaining completely from wine, commenting, "Wine and women make the wise apostatise." However, the priest was never idle and spent his time praying, preaching, studying, administering the Sacraments and sometimes painting pictures of Christ or Our Lady. Occasionally, he would carry out exorcisms of those possessed by devils and was viewed by all Catholics in the region as an oracle to help settle arguments. Bravely he would often walk through his enemy's midst if it was necessary, joking with those who urged him to be more cautious. In fact, he disliked concealment to such a degree that he once chided some gentry who attended Mass covered up to their eyes in an effort to avoid being recognised by any spies or infiltrators possibly present: "I like not those that will be peeping at God."

Some months before his final capture (for he had been apprehended several times before) he had heard that some dear friends of his had resolved to carry out a wicked deed that would affect many souls adversely. On hearing the news, Ambrose fitted violently and lost the use of one side of his body, putting his life in danger. His burden was made worse by the fear that the flock who he had won for Christ would be left without a guide. Moreover, despite his violent convulsions and near death, no priest could be found to deliver the last rites. In these extremities he found the comfort of God:

"Lord, Thy will be done; a due conformity of our will to Thine, is to be preferred to the use of the sacraments, and even to martyrdom itself. I reverence and earnestly desire

> *"I tell you plainly that if by that unjust law you sentence me to die, it will be to my salvation and your damnation."*

(left) St. Ambrose Barlow's hand. Stanbrook Abbey, Callow End, Worcester WR2 4TD. Tel: 01905 830 209. www.stanbrookabbey.org.uk

*(far left)The wooden bust of St. Ambrose Barlow was brought from France to England by a captain from Hull in the early 19th century. It was then used as a doll by children in Blyth, Northumberland. In 1929 it was given to Abbot Ambrose Bamford of Douai after he had come across some children playing with it. The name 'A. Barlow' could originally be read on the volume on which the bust rests, and the heart-shaped cavity once contained a relic of the martyr.*

Thy sacraments; and I have often wished to lay down my life for Thee, in the profession of my faith; but if it be pleasing to Thy infinite wisdom, by this illness to take me out of the prison of this body half dead already, Thy will be done."

However, a Jesuit eventually arrived and the pervasive worry gradually subsided. It is said that when Barlow helped Fr. Arrowsmith, he had received a vision that he would be the next to suffer.

On Maundy Thursday, Ambrose was joined at Morley Hall by many Catholics from a vast area and passed the night in the same way that the Early Church used to do - watching and praying. All through the night, Ambrose heard confessions. The following day, he and the wealthier

Catholics present served dinner to the poorer ones and dined on their leftovers. When the time came to send them home, the priest gave each person a groat as alms, as well as distributing to the poor any further leftovers. Such zeal meant that he was famed throughout the area and his friends often reprimanded him for going about so publicly. His response was simply to say, "Let them fear that have anything to lose, which they are unwilling to part with." Barlow wanted nothing in this world and refused all advice to stay far away from the parish. Instead, he retired to the house of a kinsman of his in Cheshire, desiring that if God willed his blood to be spilled, then it would be in Lancaster.

Ambrose was still weak from his illness when he was apprehended for the fifth and final time on Easter Day, 25th April, 1641. A minister (the Vicar of Eccles) near the house in which he was staying had urged his large congregation on that holy day to follow him and apprehend the famous Popish priest Ambrose Barlow, who they were sure to find amidst the Catholic flock. Apparently, this was more appropriate than prayers and preaching on this day. The minister informed them that if they stayed till the end of the service then they would miss the opportunity of catching this infamous papist. The 400-strong congregation relished the proposition and armed themselves with clubs and swords. Following the parson, who marched at their head, still attired in his surplice, they reached the house. Having just finished saying Mass, Ambrose was advising a crowd of about 100 on the subject of patience. Realising that the house was surrounded, the Catholics within urged the trapped priest to hide but he refused to leave them to the mercy of the mob. Instead, he exhorted them to remain true to their faith, reminding them that such tribulations would stand them in good stead before the Lord. Informing them that he was ready to suffer for his faith, he ordered them to open the doors.

Without hesitation the rabble rushed in, screaming for Ambrose. Seeing the priest, they grabbed him and held

*continues on page 78*

> *"Let them fear that have anything to lose, which they are unwilling to part with."*

him securely. The other Catholics were allowed to leave, although their attendance was noted. Whilst all this was going on, others of the horde searched the house, breaking open Ambrose's chest in the hope of finding some money. However, although there was a significant sum of money there - that a wealthy gentleman had recently sent the priest for distribution amongst the poor - the intruders failed to discover the bag of money, despite rifling through every possession of the priest's. Ambrose later gave orders for how this money was to be distributed.

Disappointed at their lack of bounty, the mob was led by the minister (who seemingly possessed no warrant) to a Justice of the Peace on the same day. From there, Ambrose was sent to Lancaster gaol under the watch of 60 armed men. Despite some of his flock planning to rescue him, the wretched priest urged them to attempt nothing. The armed mob carried him to his prison in a triumphal procession, the rabble openly abusing and insulting him, treating him with the utmost contempt. Remarkably, Ambrose took joy from their abuse but was becoming rapidly weaker - he could not even sit on horseback without someone behind him as support.

However, despite being imprisoned from Easter till the summer assizes, the priest somehow recovered his strength. He dissuaded his friends from using any leverage to have him transported to London, as he desired to die for the cause; he reasoned that he had to die at some time and what better way to do so than for the Lord's Church. It was at this time that he told a select number about his vision of Fr. Edmund Arrowsmith, including his brother. William Rudesind Barlow, in a manuscript on his brother's life, quoted from a letter he received from Ambrose whilst he was still in prison, dated 17th May, 1641, in which he claimed that Fr. Arrowsmith, "the night before he suffered, when as yet Mr. Barlow had not heard of his suffering, came to his bedside, and told him: 'I have already suffered; you shall also suffer; speak but little, for they will be upon the watch to catch you in your words'."

During his incarceration, Ambrose often read from Boetius' *De Consolatione* until the gaoler confiscated it from him. However, the priest simply smiled and commented, "If you take this little book away, I will betake myself to that great book from which Boetius learned his wholesome doctrine, and that book you can never take away from me." Thus, he continually prayed and when visited would not discuss worldly issues but only religious ones.

After four months of being held in this way, Ambrose was brought to trial on 7th September before Sir Robert Heath, who it is believed had received instructions from Parliament that any priest caught in Lancashire was to be executed to serve as a warning to the many who were still Catholics there. Ambrose freely acknowledged that he was a priest and that he had carried out his mission in the country for over 20 years. When asked why he had not left the country according to the king's proclamation of the previous year, he replied that even those who had 'cap-

tured' him knew he was too weak to have obeyed the order. The judge pressed him on his views of the law, prompting Ambrose to respond that all laws against Catholics on account of their religion were unjust and impious, "for what law can be more unjust than this, by which priests are condemned to suffer as traitors, merely because they are Roman, that is, true priests? For there are no other true priests but the Roman, and if these be destroyed what must become of the Divine law when none remain to preach God's Word and administer His sacraments."

"Then what opinion have you of the makers of those laws, and of those who by their office see them put in execution?" pressed the Judge.

"If, my Lord," began the priest, "in consequence of so unjust a law, you should condemn me to die, you would send me to heaven and yourself to hell."

"Make what judgement you please," retorted the Judge, "of my salvation, for my part, though the law has brought you hither as a criminal and a seducer of the people, I shall not pass so uncharitable a sentence upon you."

"I am no seducer, but a reducer of the people to the true and ancient religion," was Ambrose's triumphant reply.

The judge was amazed at the constancy and bravery of the priest's answers, reminding him that he held the priest's life in his hands: "Don't you know and acknowledge that I sit here as your judge?"

"I know," replied the prisoner, "and acknowledge you judge, but in such cases only as belong to the temporal court and tribunal; but in spiritual matters, and in things belonging to the court of conscience, be pleased to take notice that I am judge, and therefore I tell you plainly that if by that unjust law you sentence me to die, it will be to my salvation and your damnation."

Disgruntled and shocked, the judge directed the jury to find him guilty. This they did and the following day the judge sentenced him to death. Hearing this, the priest gave thanks to God and then prayed heartily for God to forgive all those who had somehow been an accessory in bringing about his death. Seeing such charity, the judge granted Ambrose his one wish; that for the rest of his life he be allowed to reside in a chamber in Lancaster Castle where he could prepare for his death without any interruption.

On Friday 10th September, 1641, he was laid on the hurdle and drawn to the place of execution, carrying with him all the way a small wooden cross he had made. Reaching the place, he walked round the gallows three times, holding the cross to his chest and reciting the *Miserere*. Some ministers attempted to dispute with him about religion but he told them that now was not the time for him to entertain their follies - he had more important business to complete.

*According to sentence, Ambrose was hanged, drawn and quartered at the age of 55 and in the 24th year of his priesthood and mission. As already mentioned, a number of his relics still exist as well as his skull and a hand can be seen at Stanbrook Abbey near Worcester.*

# Alban Roe OSB, Tyburn, 1642

Born in Bury St. Edmund's, Suffolk to a Protestant family in 1583, Bartholomew Roe was known as Fr. Alban during his priesthood. He attended Cambridge University and during his time there went to visit some friends at St. Albans. There he was told of an inhabitant of the town called David who had been thrown into prison for recusancy. Alban was eager to go and talk to the prisoner, confident that he could convince him of his errors in following the Catholic faith; after all, Alban was a quick-witted man and was well versed in the alleged falsehoods professed by the Catholic faith. Therefore, Alban visited the prisoner who, despite being a mechanic, was widely read in books concerning religious issues and was able to hold his own against the young University student, even managing to go on the offensive about several articles of faith. Thus, Alban, who had been so sure of victory, left in a confused state of mind about his own religion.

This uneasiness continued unabated until Alban went to visit some Catholic priests to ask their advice. Talking to them, he learned the truth about the Catholic faith and realised the error of his ways. Having discovered the truth for himself, the young Alban was eager to share it with others so resolved to go abroad and train as a priest. Having been reconciled to the Church, he travelled to Flanders and entered into the English College of Douai. After a couple of years though, he left that establishment after being dismissed on a disciplinary matter (probably involving the headstrong temperament he had previously displayed at St. Alban's) and travelled to Dieulouard (Dieuleward, now Ampleforth) in Lorraine, where he entered the English Benedictine monastery in 1613. Having completed his year-long probation, he was admitted to his solemn profession and was

soon presented to holy orders. Shortly after his ordination, Alban's superiors felt that he was thoroughly qualified for the job ahead and sent him upon the English mission in 1615.

Arriving back in England, Alban took great pains in preaching and conferring with Protestants, converting many. After some time, he was captured by the pursuivants and committed to the New Prison, Maiden Lane, where he remained from 1618 to 1623. Thanks to the intervention of Count Gondomar, the Spanish ambassador, he and a number of other priests were released and sent into banishment after a general amnesty. Alban headed for Douai and spent about four months with his brethren at the monastery of St. Gregory, before defiantly resolving to return to England.

After another two years of labouring with great conviction, Alban was again captured in 1625. He was confined to a filthy cell at a prison in St. Albans, the very place where he had first been made aware of the truth of the Catholic Church. The authorities ensured that the terms of his confinement were very strict and he was denied all necessities; so severe was this treatment that the priest thought he would die from hunger and the cold. Owing to the intervention of some friends, he was moved to the Fleet prison after several months and was better accommodated. He was imprisoned here for 17 years, all the while working amongst the other prisoners. Despite spending most of his priesthood in prison, he continually put their needs before his own, always attempting to keep their spirits high. However, he frequently suffered different illnesses but still managed to remain patient and cheerful. All those who asked for help with their prayers were still helped though, especially by the manuscripts he wrote and the translations of pious tracts that he made.

Eventually, Alban was moved to Newgate and brought to trial at the Old Bailey. The principal witness against him was a lapsed Catholic who he had previously helped. Alban insisted that he would not be tried by a jury because he did not want his blood on the hands of innocents. The judge informed him that if he refused to plead, which he was doing by default, then the punishment would be severe. Alban's reply was defiant:

"My Saviour has suffered far more for me than all that; and I am willing to suffer the worst of torments for His sake."

Disgruntled, the judge sent him back to prison to think a little more deeply on the subject.

After taking advice from some learned priests, Alban was returned to the bar and consented to be tried by jury just like so many other witnesses of Christ. The jury quickly found him guilty of high treason on account of his being a priest. Despite this, Alban remained calm, thanking the judge

*continues on page 80*

*"Thou hast often told me I should be hanged ... I see thou art a prophet!"*

and the jury for the favour they had done him. Turning to the onlookers, he announced that he was a priest and suffered for this fact alone. He then offered to discuss the Catholic faith for which he had laboured for about 30 years with anybody who desired in that open court. However, the judges thought the idea was unthinkable and sent him back to prison, taken aback by his bravery and constancy.

During the few days between his sentencing and execution, Alban seemed in a continual state of happiness. Great numbers came to visit him and all were impressed by his demeanour. Early on the morning of his execution, he found means to say Mass and afterwards gave those Catholics present his last benediction and exhorted them to remember his teachings every time they passed his head on London Bridge or another of his body parts adorning one of the city gates. The teachings he particularly implored them to remember were to hold fast to the Catholic faith and to lead a holy life.

Informed that the execution party was waiting for him, Alban walked down the steps to greet them with an edifying composure, saluting the sheriff and the awaiting multitude with great civility. Seeing the 80 year-old Fr. Thomas Greene (known as Reynolds on the Mission) already on the hurdle, Alban, in his usual jocular manner, took the priest's hand and pretended to feel for a pulse, asking Fr. Reynolds how he felt. Fr. Reynolds replied, "In very good heart, blessed be God for it, and glad that I am to have for my companion in death a person of your undaunted courage." Alban was then tied to the hurdle and the pair were drawn to Tyburn.

Alban's spirits remained high throughout the ordeal. At one point on the journey to Tyburn he even spotted one of his former prison guards, crying out cheerfully: "Thou hast often told me I should be hanged … I see thou art a prophet!"

Arriving at the place of execution, the two made their last confessions to each other, before embracing and congratulating one another. They then clambered into the cart beneath the gallows and kissed the ropes from which they were too hang. Putting on their stoles for this last sacrifice, they commended themselves to the prayers of all Catholics. Whilst Fr. Reynolds gave his final speech, Alban busied himself in preparing one of the three malefactors also in the cart who he had reconciled in prison. Fr. Reynolds finishing his oration, Alban started to speak:

"Here's a jolly company! I know you come to see me die; my fellow here hath in great measure spoke what I would have said. However, I shall repeat the words I used at the bar. I say, then, here again, for a man to be put to death for being a priest, this being the most sacred and highest order in the world, is an unjust and tyrannical law. I say, that law of the 27th of Queen Elizabeth, which condemns a man to death for being a priest only, is a wicked, unjust, and tyrannical law - a law not to be found even amongst the Turks, or elsewhere in the whole universe, England excepted."

"I must not suffer you to vilify the laws," interjected the Sheriff. "I am here to see justice done, and cannot hear you make these reflections upon the laws and judicial proceedings of the nation."

Thus, Alban was forbidden to speak any further to the assembled people. Instead, he sought to have a private word with the Sheriff.

"Pray, sir, if I will conform to your religion, and go to church, will you secure me my life?"

"That I will," confirmed the Sheriff, "upon my word; my life for yours if you will but do that."

Turning to the people, Alban announced, "See, then, what the crime is for which I am to die, and whether my religion be not my only treason."

Alban and Fr. Greene then began to pray; whilst the minister from Newgate prayed with the other convicted felons, the two priests recited the *Miserere* psalm alternately. The executioner then came to cover their faces but Alban said he had disposed of his handkerchief, commenting, "I dare look death in the face." Reportedly, he also gave the executioner money for a couple of drinks, chiding him not to get drunk.

Recommending his soul to God, the cart was drawn away. Whilst hanging, Alban visibly held his hands before his breast for a short while, twice separating them a little only to rejoin them as one employed in prayer.

After hanging till he was dead, his body was cut down and stripped for quartering. On doing this, the executioner discovered a page of writing, possibly the speech that Alban intended to give before being denied that right. The Sheriff immediately requisitioned the piece of paper and is alleged to have shown it to Parliament. Its contents have never been revealed.

During the quartering, many of those present dipped their handkerchiefs in the blood of the two martyrs, whilst others gathered up the bloody straws and any other thing that could be used as a relic. Known Protestants were seen to partake in these acts, one even dipping his glove into the blood because he had no handkerchief with him at the time.

*Alban Roe suffered at Tyburn on 21st January, 1642, the two condemned priests hanging simultaneously from the same gibbet.*

# Henry Morse SJ, Tyburn, 1645

Born in 1595 to a Protestant family at Brome in Suffolk, Henry Morse was sometimes known under the alias of Cuthbert Claxton during his time on the Mission. Henry was the sixth of nine sons and his older brother, William, also became a Jesuit priest, dying in Hampshire in 1649. When Henry was 23 years-old, whilst studying law, probably at Barnard's Inns in London, he began to examine his own conscience and the arguments behind the Catholic faith. After reaching a conclusion, he went to Flanders and was received into the Church at Douai on 5th June, 1614, and prepared to begin training for the priesthood. Stepping off the boat after landing at Dover on a short return trip to England, Henry was immediately ordered to take the Oath of Supremacy. Refusing, he was left to languish in New Prison in Southwark for four years before being released in a general amnesty by King James. Heading straight back to Douai, he trained there till 15th September, 1620, at which point he journeyed to Rome, entering the English College there and completing his priestly formation.

Having been sent upon the English Mission on 19th June, 1624, Henry landed at Newcastle. However, he was greeted by the authorities and taken before a magistrate on suspicion of being a priest. He was incarcerated for three years in terrible conditions amongst felons and other criminals at York prison, causing his health to deteriorate markedly. Whilst in prison, though, he made his novitiate as a Jesuit under his fellow prisoner, Fr. John Robinson SJ.

After three years had passed, in which time he had reconciled several of the imprisoned criminals to the Church, Henry was banished from England. Once back on the continent, he travelled to Watten, where he rested in the hope of recovering his health. Whilst there, he also offered support to the novices training for the priesthood. His health recovered, he was sent on a mission to the English soldiers at that time in the service of the King of Spain in the Low Countries. They were billeted nearby and Henry made great inroads amongst them. However, he contracted a fever that looked like it would kill him but, with God's grace, he survived. After once again recovering his strength, he spent time at Watten and Liege, before he decided it was time to return to England.

Thus, he returned to his homeland in 1633 and successfully laboured in London during the horrific plague year of 1636. The amount of work he got through was remarkable - visiting, assisting, comforting and relieving the poor unfortunates who were infected, whether they were Catholic or Protestant. He even made a list of 400 infect-

ed families that he visited in turn. So charitable were these acts, and unheard of at the time, that many Protestants converted after seeing Henry's example, naming him the 'Priest of the Plague'. Despite being infected three times with this dreaded disease, he still survived, even though it looked like the last bout would finish him off. However, he revived on receiving a letter from his superior that advised him to rest from his mission amongst the sick.

Not long after receiving this letter, he was apprehended on 27th February, 1638, by a special warrant from the Lords of the Privy Council and committed to Newgate. He was brought to trial at the next assizes and accused of being a priest, as well as attempting to seduce His Majesty's subjects to Catholicism. A certificate was brought to the court that showed Henry had converted 560 Protestants in and about the parish of St. Giles-in-the-Fields alone. Although this could not be legally proved, it demonstrates the reputation he had for reconciling Protestants. However, the jury found him guilty of being a priest but he was bailed after the personal intervention of Queen Henrietta Maria, King Charles I's Catholic wife. Shortly after, Henry was sent into banishment under the king's proclamation that all priests in the country had to leave before 7th April, 1640, particularly as he was unwilling to embarrass his bail bondsman by not obliging to the demand.

Back on the continent, Henry again missioned amongst the English soldiers. This time it was in Henry Gage's regiment, who were fighting the Dutch in Spain; so great was Henry's zeal that the Colonel greatly admired him, always referring to him as 'the holy Father'. However, still he desired to return to England, where there was a larger 'field' to work in and a better chance of winning the crown of martyrdom. Thus, he pestered his superiors until they agreed. He was in Ghent when he heard the longed for news in 1643. Knowing that this may bring his death, he went from room to room bidding farewell to his colleagues before joyfully sailing to the North of England.

Landing safely, he worked diligently amongst the Catholic population there for a year and a half. Whilst travelling to a sick person's house on the Cumberland border, he was arrested under suspicion of being a priest by a band of Roundhead soldiers who were on the lookout for someone else. He was sent under guard to Durham and spent one night of the journey at a constable's house. However, the constable's wife was a Catholic and she managed to help the priest escape.

*continues on page 82*

About six weeks later, it seemed God willed him to suffer for his faith. Travelling in Durham, Henry was being guided by a local to a house, when, one or two miles from their goal, the guide suddenly became lost. Unable to remember the way, the two travellers decided to knock on the door of a nearby cottage to ask directions. Unfortunately, the owner of the house recognised Henry as the person who had recently escaped some soldiers. Unwilling to lie, the shocked priest confirmed the man's suspicions and he was quickly taken and thrown into Durham gaol. For several weeks he was held in a filthy cell before being carried to Newcastle for shipping to London.

Throughout the voyage, the ship's crew continually abused the poor priest. Moreover, Henry thought they would all perish in a storm in which he saw another ship sunk, but he was preserved for a more glorious end. On 24th January, he arrived in London and was sent to Newgate prison. Despite his brother, an eminent lawyer and Protestant, attempting everything to save Henry's life, the priest was brought to the bar on 30th January and found guilty of being the same priest who had been banished before. Thus, no further trial was needed and Henry was sent back to Newgate to await his execution for high treason. During this time, many people visited him and were greatly moved by his saintly behaviour.

1st February, 1645, was the day of his execution. Early in the morning he celebrated a votive Mass of the Holy Trinity in thanksgiving for the great blessing God had rewarded him. He also recited the litanies of Our Lady and all the saints for the conversion of England. After this, he made an exhortation to the Catholics present, before retiring to solitary prayer for an hour. This completed, he then visited each of his fellow prisoners and cheerfully bade them farewell, much to their astonishment. For the short time that remained, he and another Jesuit prayed in private. Informed that the time had come, Henry fell to his knees, lifted his hands and eyes to heaven, and gave thanks to

at Tyburn begged for the priest's prayers in bringing peace to Christendom, as well as for the king and kingdom of France. The Count D'Egmont was also present in the coach and took his leave of the priest, as did the Portuguese ambassador. Without further pause, Henry climbed into the cart under the gallows and addressed the crowd.

"I am come hither to die for my religion, for that religion which is professed by the Catholic Roman Church, founded by Christ, established by the Apostles, propagated through all ages by a hierarchy always visible to this day, grounded on the testimonies of holy scriptures; upheld by the authorities of fathers and councils, out of which, in fine, there can be no hopes of salvation."

The sheriff interrupted him, bidding him to speak no further on that subject. Instead, he advised him to tell of any plots he knew to kill the king or the whole of Parliament. Henry replied calmly, "I have a secret which highly concerns his Majesty and Parliament," prompting the crowd to fall silent in expectation. "Gentlemen, take note. The kingdom of England will never be truly blessed until it returns to the Catholic faith."

Ignoring the shocked murmurings of the crowd, Henry defiantly continued:

"The time was when I was a Protestant, being then a student of the laws in the Inns of Court in town; till being suspicious of the truth of my religion I went abroad into Flanders, and upon full conviction renounced my former errors, and was reconciled to the Church of Rome, the mistress of all churches. Upon my return into England I was committed to prison for refusing the oath of pretended allegiance; and from prison, though I was then no priest, I was sent into banishment. I went to Rome, and after I had gone through the course of my studies for seven years I returned into England to help the souls of my neighbours; and here amongst other charities, I devoted myself to the service of the poor Catholics and others in the time of the

> "I am come hither to die for my religion, for that religion which is professed by the Catholic Roman Church, founded by Christ, established by the Apostles, propagated through all ages by a hierarchy always visible to this day, grounded on the testimonies of holy scriptures."

God, offering himself as a sacrifice to His Divine Majesty.

"Come, my sweetest Jesu, that I may now be inseparably united to Thee in time and in eternity! Welcome ropes, hurdles, gibbets, knives, and butchery! Welcome for the love of Jesus my Saviour!"

At 9am, the sheriff came for Henry and led him to the awaiting sledge, which was to be pulled by four horses. On his journey to the scaffold, the French ambassador, who said that he craved Henry's benediction, openly saluted the priest. The ambassador then followed in his coach and

late plague, and suffered nothing to be wanting that lay in me to their spiritual comfort."

The sheriff and a Protestant minister castigated the brave priest, telling him not to boast of his good deeds, prompting Henry into a response.

"I will glory in nothing but in my infirmities; but all glory I ascribe to God who was pleased to make use of so weak an instrument in so pious a ministry; and who is pleased now to favour me so far as to allow me this day to seal the Catholic faith with my blood; a favour which I have begged

# TYBURN
## The King's Gallows

> *"Gentlemen, take note. The kingdom of England will never be truly blessed until it returns to the Catholic faith."*

of Him for these thirty years. And I pray that my death may be some kind of atonement for the sins of this nation; and if I had as many lives as there are sands in the sea, I would most willingly lay them all down for this end, and in testimony of the Catholic faith, which faith is the only true, the only certain faith, the only faith confirmed by miracles still continuing; in which to this day the blind see, the dumb speak, the dead are raised to life. For thy testimonies, O Lord, are made credible exceedingly.

"But as, Mr. Sheriff, you were pleased to ask if I knew of any plots against the King or Parliament, I here declare sincerely, in the presence of God, I never in my life had knowledge of any such plot or conspiracy, much less was I myself ever engaged in any. And I hold for certain that the present tumults, and all the calamities under which the nation groans, are to be ascribed to nothing else but heresy, and the spawn of so many sects; and that it will be in vain to look for tranquility and happiness, or any lasting remedy for these evils, as long as this mortal poison remains in the very bowels of the nation."

Infuriated, the sheriff stopped Morse from speaking any further, advising him to prepare for his imminent death.

"I will do as you bid me," replied the priest, "and will prepare myself as well as I can for my departure hence, which is indeed the thing I have been doing for these 30 years, ever since I was a Catholic."

Composing himself, he prayed in a loud voice to the Holy Trinity, acknowledging himself to be a grave sinner, humbly begging mercy for his offences. Furthermore, he forgave his enemies and persecutors and hoped that God would do the same. He also prayed for all Christian kingdoms, especially England before recommending his soul to God in the words of the dying Jesus: "Into Thy hands, O Lord, I commend my spirit."

As he finished speaking, the cart was drawn away from under him. He hanged till he died quietly. During the quartering, the footmen of the French Ambassador and the Count D'Egmont dipped their handkerchiefs in the martyr's blood. His quarters were displayed on four of the city gates, whilst his head was placed on London Bridge for all to see.

*Henry Morse suffered on 1st February, 1645, after 50 years of adventure-filled life.*

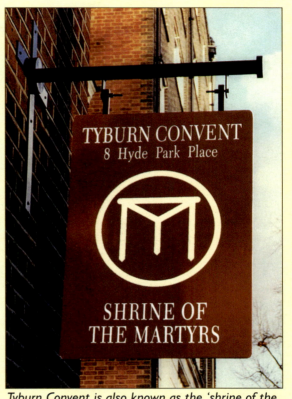

*Tyburn Convent is also known as the 'shrine of the martyrs' for it marks the spot near Marble Arch where the King's Gallows stood from 1196-1783. Nearly half of the canonised martyrs of England and Wales were amongst the 105 Catholic martyrs executed here.*

*The Martyrs' altar represents the infamous triple gallows established at Tyburn.*

# John Southworth, priest, Tyburn, 1654

The youngest son of a branch of the Southworth family of Samlesbury Hall in Preston, John Southworth was born in Lancashire in 1592. He came from a staunchly Catholic family and his father, a knight, had been fined repeatedly for refusing to attend Protestant services. Furthermore, he also spent some time in prison for harbouring Edmund Campion at Samlesbury Hall.

John was educated at the English College of Douai and was also ordained there before being sent on the English Mission on 13th October, 1619.

Initially, the priest laboured in his native Lancashire for some years before being caught and sentenced to death for being a priest in 1627. However, he was reprieved but still remained as a prisoner in Lancaster Castle. The following year, it was John who gave the last rites to Edmund Arrowsmith as he was being taken away for execution.

By April 1630, John had been taken to London and incarcerated at the Clink but was released on 11th April, 1630, with 15 other priests and delivered to the Marquis de Chasteauneuf, the French ambassador, to be transported abroad. If John did obey his exile order, he certainly did not do so for any great length of time as he was soon back, working diligently at his vocation.

During the period after his first arrest, John was known to frequent the plague-ridden streets of Westminster whilst he lived at Clerkenwell, most likely working with Henry Morse. Not only did he minister to known Catholics (relief for the destitute and infected was provided by special assessments in the parishes, but known Catholics were ineligible for this aid) but he also converted many Protestants. For example, he visited the house of William Baldwin and William Stiles in the Kemp Yard at Westminster. Baldwin was close to death but before he passed away, John reconciled him to the Catholic Church. Stiles also converted at the same time.

*(above) Samlesbury Hall.*
*(right) St. John Southworth's remains now rest in Westminster Cathedral.*

Moreover, he converted many other poor people, who frequented Masses that he held at Denmark House. The kind priest was also known to bring food to the living trapped inside infected houses, shut in there to prevent the disease from spreading.

In 1637 he seems to have taken up residence in Westminster, where he was arrested on 28th November and sent to the Gatehouse. From there, he was again transferred to the Clink and in 1640 was brought before the Commissioners for Causes Ecclesiastical, who returned him to prison on 24th June. On 16th July, he was again liberated but by 2nd December, he was back in the Gatehouse. Finally, in 1654, John was caught for the last time upon the information of a pursuivant called Jeffries. The priest was dragged from his bed one night by Colonel Worsley and confessed that he had been exercising his priestly functions since his reprieve. John was tried at the Old Bailey and the usual persuasive promises offered but the 62 year-old priest stood firm, refusing to deny that he was a priest; to do so would have been to deny his faith. Reluctantly, the Recorder of London, Sergeant Steel, condemned him to death.

Finally, on 28th June, 1654, the elderly John was dragged to Tyburn upon a sledge. Despite the stormy and rainy weather, thousands appeared to watch his execution, including a number of wealthy people seated in horse-drawn carriages. John made a lengthy speech beneath the gallows whilst wearing his vestments and a four-cornered cap:

"Good people, I was born in Lancashire. This is the third time I have been apprehended, and now being to die, I would gladly witness and profess openly my faith for which I suffer. And though my time be short, yet what I shall be deficient in words I hope I shall supply with my blood, which I will most willingly spend to the last drop for my faith. Neither my intent in coming into England, nor practice in England, was to act anything against the secular government. Hither I was sent by my lawful superiors to teach Christ's faith, not to meddle with any temporal affairs. Christ sent His apostles; His apostles their successors; and their successors me. I did what I was commanded by them, who had power to command me, being ever taught that I ought to obey them in matters ecclesiastical, and my temporal governors in business only temporal. I never acted nor thought and hurt against the current Protector. I had only a care to do my own obligation, and discharge my own duty in saving my own and other men's souls. This, and only this, according to my poor abilities, I laboured to perform. I had commission to do it from him, to whom our Saviour, in His predecessor St. Peter, gave power to send others to propagate His faith. This is that for which I die, O, holy cause! and not for any treason against the laws. My faith and obedience to my superiors is all the treason charged against me; nay, I die for Christ's law, which no human law, by whomsoever made, ought to withstand or contradict. This law of Christ commanded me to obey these superiors, and this Church, saying, whoever hears them hears Himself. This Church, these superiors of it I obeyed, and for obeying, die. I was brought up in the truly ancient Roman Catholic apostolic religion, which taught me that the sum of the only true Christian profession is to die. This lesson I have heretofore in my lifetime desired to learn; this lesson I come here to put in practice by dying, being taught it by our Blessed Saviour, both by precept and example. Himself said, 'He that will be My disciple, let him take up his cross and follow Me.' Himself exemplary, practised what he had recommended to others. To follow His holy doctrine, and imitate His holy death, I willingly suffer at present; this gallows [looking up] I look on as His cross which I gladly take to follow my dear saviour. My faith is my crime, the performance of my duty the occasion of my condemnation. I confess I am a great sinner; against God I have offended, but am inno-

cent of any sin against man; I mean the Commonwealth and present Government. How justly then I die, let them look to who have condemned me. It is sufficient for me that it is God's will: I plead not for myself - I came hither to suffer - but for you poor persecuted Catholics whom I leave behind me. Heretofore liberty of conscience was pretended as a cause of war; and it was held a reasonable proposition that all the natives should enjoy it, who should be found to behave themselves as obedient and true subjects. This being so, why should their conscientious acting and governing themselves, according to the faith received from their ancestors, involve them more than all the rest in any universal guilt which conscientiousness is the very reason that clears others, and renders them innocent? It has pleased God to take the sword out of the King's hand and put it in the Protector's. Let him remember that he is to administer justice indifferently, and without exceptions of persons. For there is no exception of persons with God whom we ought to resemble. If any Catholics work against the present Government let them suffer; but why should all the rest who are guiltless - unless conscience be their guilt - be made partakers in a promiscuous punishment with the greatest malefactors? The first rebellion was of the angels; the guilty were cast into hell, the innocent remained partakers of the heavenly blessings."

Some of the surrounding officers then ordered him to hurry up so, after requesting that any Catholics who were present pray for him, he shut his eyes and prayed silently, awaiting his inevitable fate.

Five counterfeiters were hanged, drawn and quartered with him.

One of the Howard family of Norfolk sent the dead priest's mangled body over to the English College of Douai, where it was deposited in the church, near St. Augustine's altar. Famously, prayers said before the saint's relics led to the cure of Francis Howard, (the fifth son of Henry, Earl of Arundel, who was the brother of both Thomas and Henry, Dukes of Norfolk), who had been given up for dead by all the doctors who saw him.

*During the French Revolution, the saint's relics were hidden and not re-discovered until 1927. They are now enshrined in Westminster Cathedral.*

# John Plessington, priest, Chester, 1679

**B**orn at Dimples Hall near Garstang, Lancashire in 1637, John was the son of Robert Plessington, who had been governor for the king at Greenhalgh Castle during the Civil War and, as such, had suffered imprisonment and the loss of his estates for this loyalty.

John attended a Jesuit-run private school in Scarisbrick Hall, near Ormskirk, and thus adopted the alias 'Scarisbrick' on entering the English College of St. Alban the martyr in Valladolid on 18th November, 1660. He was ordained in Segovia on 25th March, 1662.

Returning to England in 1663, John chiefly resided with the Massey family of Puddington Hall in Cheshire, carrying out most of his missionary work in Holywell and around Chester. During his time with the family, he posed as the children's teacher. However, because of his success in reclaiming souls, he angered a number of people. Problems came to a head when he opposed the marriage of a wealthy Catholic woman to a Protestant gentleman, prompting the man's family to seek revenge by reporting him to the authorities. Thus, he was apprehended and imprisoned in Chester Castle.

He was brought to trial there in May 1679 upon an indictment of high treason as part of the Oates Plot, as well as for having become a Catholic priest and, finally, for staying in the country, which was contrary to the 27th statute of Elizabeth's reign. Margaret Platt, George Massey and Robert Wood testified against him, swearing that they had seen him exercise his priestly functions. Upon their evidence, John was found guilty and sentenced to death, despite his valid point that Platt was insane and Massey was a notorious liar, meaning they actually only had one witness when two were necessary by law. It is of note that all the witnesses led miserable lives after providing their false witness – one was crushed to death in an accident, another died in a pigsty whilst the last suffered in pain and misery until death.

After his condemnation, the 42 year-old priest was imprisoned for nine weeks before being drawn to the place of execution – Gallows Hill to the west of Chester (now called Barrel Well Hill) - on 19th July, 1679. Despite the sentence against him, the authorities followed their usual red tape, an undertaker arriving to measure John for a coffin just prior to his execution. Whilst this pointless act was going on, a friend arrived at the prison to visit the condemned priest, John joking to him, "I'm ordering my last suit."

At Gallows Hill, John spoke to the people as follows:

"Dear countrymen, I am here to be executed, neither for theft, murder, nor anything against the law of God; nor any fact or doctrine inconsistent with monarchy or civil government. I suppose several now present heard my trial at last assizes and can testify that nothing was laid to my charge but priesthood. I am sure that you will find that priesthood is neither against the law of God nor monarchy, nor civil government, if you will consult either the Old or New Testament [for it is the basis of religion]; for no priest no religion, St. Paul tells us in Hebrews 7:12. The priest-

*Scarisbrick Hall near Ormskirk.*

hood being changed, there is made of necessity a change of the law, and consequently the priesthood being abolished, the law and religion is quite gone.

"But I know it will be said that a priest ordained by authority derived from the See of Rome is by the law of the nation to die as a traitor. But if that be so, what must become of all the clergymen of the Church of England? The first Protestant bishops had their ordination from those of the Church of Rome, or none at all, as appears by their own writers; so that ordination comes thence derivatively to those now living.

"As in the primitive times, Christians were esteemed traitors and suffered as such by national laws, so are the priests of the Roman Church here esteemed and suffer as such. But as Christianity then was not against the law of God, monarchy or civil policy, so now there is not any one point of the Roman Catholic faith – of which faith I am – that is inconsistent therewith, as is evident by induction in each several point.

"That the Pope hath power to depose or give license to murder princes is no point of our belief. And I protest in the sight of God and the court of heaven that I am absolutely innocent of the plot so much discoursed of, and abhor such bloody and damnable designs. Although it be nine weeks since I was sentenced to death, there is not anything of that laid to my charge, so that I may well take comfort in St. Peter's words (First Letter, 4:15-16): 'Let none of you suffer as a murderer, or as a thief, or as an evil-doer, or as a mischief-maker; yet if any suffer as a Christian, let him not be ashamed or sorry.' I have deserved a worse death, for although I have been a faithful and true subject to my king, I have been a grievous sinner against God. Thieves and robbers that rob on highways would have served God in a greater perfection than I have done, had they received so many favours and graces from Him as I have.

"But as there was never a sinner who truly repented and heartily called to Jesus for mercy to whom He did not show mercy, so I hope, by the merits of His Passion, He will have mercy on me, who am heartily sorry that I ever offended Him.

"Bear witness, good hearers, that I profess that I undoubtedly and firmly believe all the articles of the Roman Catholic faith, and for the truth of any of them, by the assistance of God, I am willing to die; and I had rather die than doubt of any point of faith taught by our holy Mother the Roman Catholic Church.

"In what condition Margaret Platt, one of the chiefest witnesses against me, was before and after she was with me, let her nearest relations declare.

"George Massey, another witness, swore falsely when he swore I gave him the sacrament and said Mass at the time and place he mentioned. I verily think that he never spoke to me, or I to him, or saw each other but at the assizes week. The third witness, Robert Wood, was suddenly killed; but of the dead, why should I speak? These were all the witnesses against me, unless those only declared what they heard from others. I heartily and freely forgive all that have been or are any way instrumental to my death, and heartily desire that those that are living may heartily repent.

"God bless the King and the royal family, and grant His Majesty a prosperous reign here, and a crown of glory hereafter. God grant peace to the subjects, and that they live and die in true faith, hope and charity. That which remains is that I recommend myself to the mercy of my Jesus, by whose merits I hope for mercy. O Jesu, be to me a Jesus."

Having said his last words, John was turned off the ladder to be hanged, before being stripped and quartered.

Local tradition claims that the four quarters of his body were then sent to Puddington Hall with an order that they be exhibited in each of the corners of the house to act as a reminder of what happened to 'traitors'. However, the people of the area would not allow it, instead placing the pieces on an oak table in the entrance of the house. Finally, they were buried in the cemetery at Burton.

# Philip Evans SJ, Cardiff, 1679

# John Lloyd, priest, Cardiff, 1679

**B**orn in Monmouthshire in 1645, Philip Evans was educated at St. Omer's before entering the Society of Jesus on 7th September 1665, when he was 20 years-old. After completing his noviceship with great aplomb, he was ordained at Liege and sent upon the English Mission in 1675. Assigned to South Wales, he diligently worked for the cause for four years, gaining many souls for the Church and fearing no dangers where the glory of God and his neighbour's salvation were at stake. When the fierce persecution that followed the Oates' Plot 'broke out', Philip was advised by some friends to go into hiding because his zeal and work had made him so famous in the area. However, the priest refused and chose to risk his life for his flock like a good shepherd rather than run away and leave them to the wolves.

Not long after this, he was captured at the house of Christopher Turberville at Sker, Glamorganshire by Justice Logher on 4th December, 1678. When he refused to take the Oath of Allegiance, he was promptly thrown into Cardiff Castle gaol, where he was kept in solitary confinement in a dungeon for three weeks. His silence was eventually broken when Brecon-born Fr. John Lloyd was committed to the same cell and remained his companion until death. John had taken his mission oath at the Royal College of St. Alban in Valladolid on 16th October, 1649 and had laboured among the hills and valleys of Brecon and Monmouth for 24 years. He was captured at the house of a Mr. Turberville at Penllyn, Glamorganshire on 20th November, 1678. However, Philip and John had to wait a considerable time for their sentence, as it took five months to induce anyone to appear as a witness against them, two men even being flogged because they refused to say that they had seen the priests saying Mass. The chief witness against Philip was an apostate named Mayne Trott. He was deformed, and had been a dwarf at the Spanish and British Courts, but was at this time in the service of John Arnold of Abergavenny, an indefatigable

*Philip Evans.*

priest-hunter, who had offered a £200 award for the capture of any priest. Eventually, a mother and daughter were harassed into testifying against John but that the trial was a sham was not even disguised. John's captor, Richard Bassett, was unbelievably sitting on the jury and when the judge ordered the jury to find the priest

*continues on page 88*

guilty of treason if they believed the evidence put before them, the irascible Bassett shouted, "You can leave that to us. By God, we shall find him guilty." Both priests were swiftly pronounced guilty by the jury of the high treason of priesthood when they were brought to the Bar on 5th May, 1679.

When the sentence was announced, Philip bowed in thanks to the judge and with great joy was returned to gaol with his former companion, also sentenced to death on the same day. However, the execution was delayed for a lengthy period; so long, that many thought the pair were to be reprieved. They were even allowed out of prison for some recreation during this time! Eventually, orders arrived without warning that they were to die the following day.

At the time, Philip and John were on release and playing tennis. When the gaoler came to find them and return the pair to prison, Philip responded in an untroubled manner, "What haste is there? Let me first play out my game." This he did and on returning to prison, the condemned priest took up his harp and played for joy at the victory that would soon be won by his dying for the Faith. Shortly after, Philip's feet were bound in chains that he happily kissed. Many Catholics began to flock to the prison and he took the chance to exhort them to constancy in their faith and patience in their sufferings.

At nine o'clock on the morning of 22nd July 1679, the Under-Sheriff, Charles Evans, came to the dungeon where the condemned pair were housed. A smith was sent for to remove the priests' chains but Philip's were fastened so tight that it took an hour for them to be removed, causing great pain to the poor priest. On being brought from the dungeon, both priests requested that they walk to the place of execution but this was denied and they were brought upon a cart. Their arms were pinioned yet they still managed to read their prayer books.

Arriving at the place of death, Gallows Field (now the northern end of Richmond Road in Cardiff), both priests followed St. Andrew's example, saying, "Welcome, good cross", before falling to their knees and kissing the gallows. After praying like this for a while, the Sheriff told them that Philip was to die first. Bowing to the crowd, he started his oration:

"I need not tell you why we were brought here to suffer; one sentence of condemnation is a sufficient witness that it was not for a plot, or any other crime but for being priests; consequently I do die for religion and conscience sake. I shall not speak much of the goodness of my cause, because I think it will be needless; but it is so good that I would not give the happiness of dying for it, for all the crowns of the world. Sure if a man ever speaks truth, it must be at the hour of death, therefore I hope nobody will doubt of what I say. If I have or had any enemies in the world, which I do not know that ever I had in my life, I do heartily forgive them for anything done or said against me; and if I have offended anybody, I am heartily sorry for it and ask them forgiveness. I say God bless and prosper the king.

I beg the prayers of all, and in particular of the Catholics here present."

Finished, Philip knelt and prayed with some companions. Bidding them farewell, he went up the ladder and again turned to address the watching crowd:

"Sure this is the best pulpit a man can have to preach in, therefore I cannot forbear to tell you again that I die for God and religion's sake; and I think myself so happy that if I had never so many lives, I would willingly give them all for so good a cause. If I could live, it would be but for a little time, though I am but young; happy am I that can purchase with a short pain an everlasting life. I do forgive all those that have had any hand in my death, accusation, or condemnation: I ask again forgiveness of everybody. I give thanks to all those that have been kind to me, and to you, Mr. Sheriff. Adieu, Mr. Lloyd, though for a little time, for we shall shortly meet again. Pray for me all; and I shall return it, when it pleaseth God that I shall enjoy the beautiful vision. If any of you that see me die thus willingly for my religion have any good thought upon it, I shall think myself happy."

Pausing, Philip then said "*In manus tuas, Domine commendo spiritum meum*." He then made the sign of the cross and was turned off the ladder by the executioner. However, his legs became entangled with the steps of the ladder so Richard Jones, one of the Sheriff's bailiffs, rushed forward and freed his legs. Thus, Philip was left to hang but, according to Catholic and Protestant reports, he had never looked happier.

During this time, John had been watching events unfold, compassionately witnessing the fate of his companion, who was still fully conscious as the executioners ripped his abdomen apart. Before it was his turn to climb the ladder, he spoke heartily to the crowd.

"My fellow-sufferer has declared the cause of our death, there I need not repeat it; and besides I never was a good speaker in my life. I shall only say that I die in the true Catholic and apostolic faith, according to these words in the creed, I believe the holy Catholic Church; and with those three virtues, faith, hope and charity. I forgive all those that have offended me; and if I have offended anybody I am heartily sorry for it and ask them forgiveness. I beg the prayers of all, and in particular of the Catholics here present, desiring them to bear their crosses patiently, and to remember that passage of Holy Scripture, 'Happy are they that suffer persecution for justice, for theirs is the kingdom of heaven'."

He then climbed the ladder and gave thanks to all who had shown him kindness, including the Sheriff. Knocking his breast three times, John proclaimed, "Lord have mercy upon me, a sinner," and "Into Thy hands, Lord, I recommend my spirit" in Latin. Giving the sign, he was then turned off the ladder.

*Philip Evans and John Lloyd suffered at Cardiff on 22nd July, 1679. Philip was aged 34 and had spent 14 of those years as a Jesuit; John was 49 years-old.*

# John Wall OFM, Worcester, 1679

Known as Fr. Joachim of St. Anne during his priesthood and executed under the name of Francis Johnson, John Wall was born in Lancashire in 1620, probably at Chingle Hall near Preston. John was born into a wealthy and staunchly Catholic family and was thus sent to the English College of Douai at a very young age. Notably, John was baptised by Edmund Arrowsmith. On 5th November, 1641, he enrolled at the English College in Rome and was ordained on 3rd December, 1645. At the age of 31, he entered the Franciscan order on New Year's Day 1651, taking his vows the following year. Due to his great zeal for regular discipline and the admiration this earned from his colleagues, within half a year John was made vicar of the monastery, before quickly becoming master of the novices.

He was sent upon the Mission in 1656 and was active chiefly in Worcestershire. He worked laboriously for the Mission for 22 years - for 12 of which he is believed to have had as his base Harvington Hall - gaining converts through his preaching and example, all the while going under the name Webb. His zeal could also be slightly impetuous, although always holy. For example, when he heard of Protestants being taken ill, he would send a Catholic to their homes to warn the Protestant of the peril in which their souls lay. In this manner, the messenger, often roused from his bed in the middle of the night, prepared the way for John. Furthermore, John was also known as a man of great patience, partly through necessity. John's contemporary biographer noted that the priest was continually tested and bothered by "some unreasonably pious women, which perpetually haunted him and therefore they were not unfittingly called by an honest man 'Mr. Webb's spirits'."

However, not long after the Oates Plot, John was apprehended 'by accident' at Rushock Court near Bromsgrove by the Sheriff's deputy, who was searching for a debtor at the time (December, 1678). The unfortunate John was carried before Sir John Packington and another Justice of the Peace. Refusing their orders to take the Oath of Allegiance and Supremacy, the priest was committed to Worcester gaol without delay. He recorded his experiences of this incarceration:

"Imprisonment, in these times especially, when none can send to their friends, nor friends come to them, is the best means to teach us how to put our confidence in God alone in all things, and then He will make His promise good, That all things shall be added to us (Luke xii), which chapter if every one would read and make good use of, a prison would be better than a palace; and a confinement for religion and a good conscience sake more pleasant than all the liberties the world could afford. As for my own part, God give me His grace, and all faithful Christians their prayers; I am happy enough. We all ought to follow the narrow way though there be many difficulties in it. It is an easy thing to run the blind way of liberty, but God deliver us from all broad, sweet ways."

After five months internment, John was finally brought to trial before Judge Atkins at Worcester on 25th April, 1679. His indictment was one of high treason for being a priest and remaining in the country. Defending himself in a prudent manner, John refused to confess or deny his priest-

*continues on page 90*

hood. Only one witness appeared against him voluntarily; another three were coerced into doing so. However, he was still found guilty by the jury and was promptly sentenced to death. On hearing this, the priest bowed low in reverence, proclaiming aloud, "Thanks be to God; God save the King; and I beseech God to bless your lordship, and all this honourable bench."

"You have spoken very well," replied the judge. "I do not intend you shall die, at least not for the present, until I know the king's further pleasure."

John recorded his reaction in his narrative:

"I was not, I thank God for it, troubled with any disturbing thoughts, either against the judge for his sentence, or the jury that gave in such a verdict, or against any of the witnesses; for I was then of the same mind, as by God's grace I ever shall be, esteeming them all the best friends to me, in all they did or said, that ever I had in my life. And I was, I thank God, so present with myself whilst the judge pronounced the sentence, that without any concern for anything in

this world, I did actually at the same time offer myself and the world to God.

"After the judge was gone from the bench, several Protestant gentlemen and others who had heard my trial came to me, though strangers, and told me how sorry they were for me. To whom with thanks I replied, that I was troubled they should grieve for me or my condition, who was joyful for it myself: for I told them I had professed this faith and religion all my lifetime, which I was as sure to be true as I was sure of the truth of God's Word, on which it was grounded; and therefore in it I deposed my soul, and eternal life and happiness; and therefore should I fear to lose my temporal life for this faith whereon my eternal life depends I should be worse than an infidel; and whosoever should prefer the life of their bodies before their faith, their religion, or conscience, they were worse than heathens.

"For my own part, I told them I was as ready, by God's grace, to die tomorrow, as I had been to receive the sentence of death today, and as willingly as if I had a grant of the great-

est dukedom."

John was returned to his prison cell and eventually sent to London with several other condemned priests for questioning about the alleged Oates Plot. He was cleared of any involvement in the fictitious conspiracy. The events in London were detailed by John in a letter to Charles Trinder, counsellor and later sergeant-at-law, dated 18th July.

"Sir, With my service I return you thanks for the 20 shillings. I am safe returned from London, whither I was sent to be examined by Mr. Oates and Bedloe, Dugdale and Prance, to see if any of them had anything against me as guilty of concerning these great disturbances of the times. I was very strictly examined by all four several times over in that month I stayed at London; and thanks be to God I was, after the last examination, publicly declared innocent and free of all plots whatever, by Mr. Bedloe, who examined me last; and he was so kind to me that he told me publicly that, if I would but comply in matter of religion, that he would pawn his life for me, that for all I was condemned, yet I should not die. I was also offered the same after my first examination, though I should have been never so guilty, if I would have done what was against my conscience. But I told them I would not buy my life at so dear a rate as to wrong my conscience. How God will please to dispose of all us that are condemned none know. Some think it is concluded we must all die; and yet because it will not appear grateful in the eyes of rational and moral men to see us die merely for conscience sake, I have been several times informed from London since I came down that, if possible, some will do their best to bring some of us, one way or other, into a plot, though we have all at London been declared innocent after strict examination. God's will be done. The greater the injury and injustice done against us by men to take away our lives, the greater our glory in eternal life before God. This is the last persecution that will be in

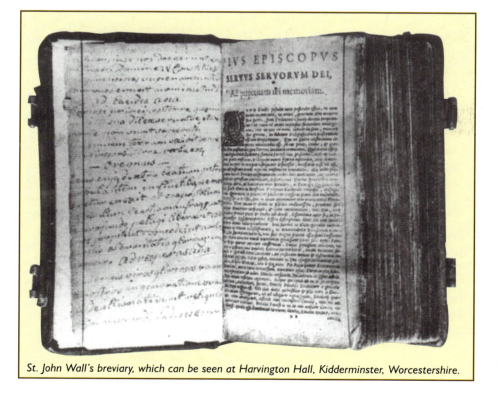
*St. John Wall's breviary, which can be seen at Harvington Hall, Kidderminster, Worcestershire.*

England; therefore I hope God will give all His holy grace to make the best use of it. All these things have been sufficiently prophesied long since; and I do no way question the truth; though it is like some will suffer first, of whom I have a strong imagination I shall be one. God's will be done in earth as it is in heaven, and in mercy bring me happy thither.

I subscribe, Sir, your faithful servant,

Francis Webb."

It is to be noted that John used his 'code name' to sign the letter. Trinder added notes at the bottom of the original letter that confirm it to definitely have been written by John.

After four months had passed since his condemnation, John was sentenced to death. Another letter is preserved by the English Franciscans of Douai dated 25th August, 1679. It is written by Fr. William Levison, who visited John during his imprisonment and witnessed the martyr's death:

"Of late I was desired, and willingly went, to visit our friend (Mr. Webb) Fr. Wall, prisoner at Worcester, whose execution drew near at hand. I came to him two days before it, and found him a cheerful sufferer of his present imprisonment, and ravished, as it were, with joy, with the future hopes of dying for so good a cause. I found, contrary in both his and my expectation, the favour of being with him alone; and the day before his execution, I enjoyed that privilege for the space of four or five hours together; during which time I heard his confession, and communicated him to his great joy and satisfaction. I ventured likewise, through his desire, to be present at his execution, and placed myself boldly next to the Under-Sheriff, near the gallows, where I had the opportunity of giving him the last absolution, just as he was turned off the ladder. During his imprisonment, he carried himself like a true servant and disciple of his crucified Master, thirsting after nothing more than the shedding of his blood for the love of his God; which he performed with a courage and cheerfulness becoming a valiant soldier of Christ, to the great edification of all Catholics, and admiration of all Protestants, the rational and moderate part especially, who showed a great sense of sorrow for his death; decrying the cruelty of putting men to death for priesthood and religion. He is the first that ever suffered at Worcester since the Catholic religion entered into this nation, which he seemed with joy to tell me before his execution. He was quartered, and his head separated from his body, according to his sentence. His body was permitted to be buried, and was accompanied by the Catholics of the town to St. Oswald's Churchyard, where he lies interred. His head I got privately, and conveyed it to Mr. Randolph, who will be careful to keep it till opportunity serves to transport it to Douai. The miseries we here lie under are great, and I hope our brothers in safety will be mindful of our condition in their best thoughts,

Just north of Preston, in the small village of Goosnargh, lies the oldest inhabited brick building in the country. Chingle Hall, formerly known as Singleton Hall, was constructed in 1260 by the knight Adam de Singleton. The Hall remained in the de Singleton family late into the 16th century. In 1585 the Wall family, who were related to the Singletons, moved into the Hall. St. John Wall was born in the Hall in 1620. In 1645 John was ordained as a priest. Throughout the period, Chingle Hall was used as a Mass centre and thus contained many priest holes and secret compartments so that people taking part in the Mass could hide if the Hall was raided by the authorities. At this time St. John Wall was extremely active, reportedly celebrating secret Masses at his birthplace on a regular basis.

and beg of God we may cheerfully bear our crosses, and, if it be His holy will, courageously sacrifice our lives in defence of our religion, which is the earnest desire of William Levison."

John suffered on Red Hill, near Worcester on 22nd August, 1679, the Octave Day of the Assumption of the Blessed Virgin. The Sheriff offered John the chance to die the following day so that he would not have to suffer the further humiliation of dying with two common criminals. However, John thanked him before telling him that if it was good enough for Jesus, then it was good enough for him.

The martyr's head was kept in the cloisters of the English Franciscans of Douai before the French Revolution. Prior to his death, John wrote a lengthy speech and passed it to a friend for printing. In it, he declared his faith, hope and charity, urging others to follow suit. Moreover, he professed his and the Catholic Church's abhorrence of all treasonous plots, imploring God's mercy for himself, the Church, the king and his kingdom, and lastly for his persecutors, who he forgave with all his heart. He finished by offering up his death to God, commending his soul into His hands. The Franciscan nuns at Taunton possess a tooth and a bone of the martyr.

## SALUTE TO FORTY MARTYRS IN ROME

Pope Paul foresees the day when Catholic and Anglican Churches will be united

THE UNIVERSE

FORTY MARTYRS: Colourful and historic issues. October 23 & 30

The Universe ran two consecutive special editions for the canonisation of the Forty Martyrs of England & Wales. Above is the front cover for the 30th October, below the 23rd October, 1970. (right) A bookstall in St. Peter's Square where pilgrims queued for their souvenir copy.

## 1535: The first of a glorious company set out for Tyburn

# The UNIVERSE

## Her cure helped Martyrs' cause

### FORTY MARTYRS' CANONISATION

This week —

## Supplement on new saints

# John Kemble, priest, Hereford, 1679

John Kemble was a member of the secular clergy and 80 years-old when he was executed. He was born at Rhyd-y-car Farm, St. Weonard's, Herefordshire in 1599. His family was Catholic and he grew up used to the company of priests, the family house allegedly being used as a Mass centre. In 1605, John's father, George, was even reported to the Privy Council for hiding a Jesuit named Stamp. Once of sufficient age, John followed his brother, the Benedictine Fr. William Walter Kemble, who had trained at the monastery of St. Gregory, to Douai College to train as a priest under the alias of Holland. John was ordained on 23rd February, 1625, sang his first Mass at 10 o'clock on the morning of 2nd March and was sent upon the Mission on 4th June, where he resided in his native county of Herefordshire. Throughout his 53 year-mission he worked with great zeal, always displaying a deep piety during his arduous travelling round the area. However, little is known of his actual activities; after all, it was not wise for a priest to advertise his whereabouts.

Eventually, he was captured by Captain John Scudamore of Kentchurch after being discovered at Pembridge Castle in West-Newton, Herefordshire, where he had been staying with his nephew during his old age. He had been warned of the approaching authorities but chose to stay, declaring that he had only a few years left to live and it would be advantageous to suffer for his religion. The captured priest was committed to Hereford gaol in November 1678 and condemned to death at the end of March, 1679. Shortly after, the aged priest was brought to London with Fr. David Lewis and held in Newgate prison whilst he was questioned by the unholy trinity of Oates, Bedloe and Dugdale about his alleged complicity in the Oates Plot, a fraudulent conspiracy to assassinate King Charles II dreamt up to increase persecution of Catholics. Unable to prove anything, they sent him back to Hereford

for three more months of imprisonment. The journey to London had been arduous for such an aged man, forced to travel most of the way slung sideways over the back of a horse. Slightly less uncomfortable but no less harsh was the return journey, when John was allowed to walk most of the 135 miles back to Hereford. He subsequently wrote to a benefactor from Hereford prison describing himself as "this poor old condemned man", excusing the delay in writing by explaining, "I have been so bruised in body that I have not been able to sit so long as to write to you."

After John's return to Hereford gaol, Scudamore's children often visited him. The captain's wife and children were Catholics and obviously felt some attachment to the aged priest, possibly having received the sacraments from him in the past. The old priest gave the children as much as he could, explaining that their father was the greatest friend he had by arresting him.

The priest was executed at Widemarsh Common, about two miles outside the city of Hereford, on 22nd August, 1679. Before leaving for his ordeal he smoked a pipe and had a final drink with the Under-Sheriff, Mr. Diggs. This event gave rise to the Herefordshire expressions 'Kemble pipe' and 'Kemble cup', which mean a parting pipe or cup. Despite his age, he was dragged to the place of execu-

*continues on page 94*

tion on a hurdle and gave his final speech below the noose in the late afternoon:

"It will be expected I should say something, but as I am an old man, it cannot be much, not having any concern in the [Oates] plot, neither indeed believing there is any. Oates and Bedloe not being able to charge me with anything when I was brought up to London, though they were with me, makes it evident that I die only for professing the old Roman Catholic religion, which was the religion that first made this kingdom Christian, and whoever intends to be saved must die in that religion. I beg of all whom I have offended, either by thought, word, or deed, to forgive me, for I do heartily forgive all those that have been instrumental or desirous of my death."

Turning to his executioner, he took him by the hand and

said, "Honest Anthony, my friend Anthony, be not afraid; do thy office, I forgive thee with all my heart, thou wilt do me a greater kindness than discourtesy." The priest drew his cap over his eyes, fell to his knees and prayed, offering himself up to God. He then informed the executioners they could carry out their job whenever they were ready. After John had thrice repeated the words "In manus tuas Domine commendo spiritum meum" ("Into Thy hands, O Lord, I commend my spirit"), the cart was drawn away.

John hanged for at least half an hour as the noose had not been correctly applied, killing him by excruciating slow strangulation. Many Protestants in the crowd said that they had never seen a man die in such a gentlemanly or Christian manner.

Once the dead priest's body was cut down, his head was cut off. His cousin, Captain Richard Kemble, who had saved Charles II's life at the Battle of Worcester, successfully begged for the body. The remains were buried at the foot of the cross in Welsh-Newton churchyard. A flat tombstone marks the martyr's grave to this day, bearing the inscription:

> J.K.
> DYED the 27th
> Of AUGUST
> ANNO DO 1679

Sometime after this, Captain Scudamore's daughter had a violently sore throat, which was deemed to be life threatening. A devout Catholic persuaded her to apply the rope that had hanged Kemble about her neck and she was immediately cured.

Other Catholics regularly visited the grave, including Mrs. Catherine Scudamore, who had been deaf for sometime. During one prayer gathering at the tomb, Catherine could not hear that the others had left so stayed on to pray further. Suddenly, she appeared at the inn to which they had retired for refreshments, crying out that she had recovered her hearing to the amazement of the group.

*John Kemble's left hand is preserved in a beautiful shrine in the church of St. Francis Xavier in Hereford. The hand was picked up by a Catholic lady at the scene of the martyrdom and she brought it home in her apron. One of her descendants who lived in Worcestershire gave it to Fr. Anderton SJ, Rector of Hereford, in 1806. The other portions of the mutilated body were interred by Sir Richard Kemble, who had saved the life of King Charles II at the Battle of Worcester. Sir Richard interred them in the cemetery at Welsh Newton. There has been a pilgrimage to the martyr's grave every year since.*

# David Lewis SJ, Usk, 1679

Born in Abergavenny, Monmouthshire in 1616, David Lewis often acted under the alias Charles Barker during his time on the Mission. He was brought up as a Protestant despite his mother, Margaret Pritchard, being Catholic and his eight siblings being brought up in that faith. Instead, David followed his father Morgan Lewis - who later converted - and attended the Royal Grammar School at Abergavenny, where his father was headmaster. David continued in his Protestantism until he became a law student in London, probably at the Middle Temple, and was reconciled to the Church in Paris at the age of 16. After the death of his parents, his uncle, a Jesuit, sent him to the English College at Rome, where he was described as "prudent and pious" in the college diaries. The *Liber Ruber* of the college also records, "Charles Baker, vere David Lewis, a South Welshman, of the county of Monmouth, aged 21, was admitted as an alumnus, November 6, 1638." He was ordained on 20th July 1642, before entering the Society of Jesus on 16th April, 1644. His first appointment was as Spiritual Director at the English College, Rome.

David was sent upon the English Mission in 1648, working in South Wales for 31 years. Throughout this time he laboured fearlessly for the cause, seeking lost sheep and being charitable towards all those in need; for this reason, he was often known as 'the father of the poor'. Furthermore, he regularly undertook long and dangerous journeys at night to visit the faithful under the cover of darkness. At the time, the Jesuits occupied two remote farmhouses known as the Cwm in Herefordshire, and it is from here that David ministered far and wide.

However, he was to be betrayed by the bigoted Calvinist magistrate and arch priest-hunter, John Arnold, who had before professed friendship. On Sunday morning, 17th November, 1678, at the break of day, six armed men stormed into Llantarnam Abbey near Newport, where David was preparing to say Mass. He was carried in a sort of triumphal procession to Abergavenny, where, in allusion to one article of Oates' fabrications, he was shown to the people as "the pretended Bishop of Llandaff", a dangerous title reinforcing Titus Oates' claim that the Pope had appointed bishops in England. The captured priest was committed to Monmouth gaol the following day. Here he was kept in solitary confinement under close watch - he was even made to pay 14 shillings a week for this pleasure!

On the snowy 13th January, 1679, he was moved from Monmouth to Usk. During the trip, the Deputy-Sheriff and chief jailer stopped at Ragland to warm themselves against the hard driving snow. During this break, David heard that Fr. Ignatius (Walter Price) lay dying about a mile away after suffering greatly from hunger, the cold and constantly moving from barn to barn in an attempt to evade the pursuing persecutors. David felt helpless and was unable to do more than merely send his best wishes to the priest concerning the fate of his soul. Three days later at Usk, where David was confined with several other Catholics imprisoned for their faith, he heard of the sad death of the other priest.

David was brought to trial at the Lenten assizes in Monmouth on 16th March, 1679. He was brought to the bar on a charge of high treason – for having become a Catholic priest and then remaining in England. Despite pleading not guilty to the charge, five or six witnesses were deployed against him, claiming that they had seen him say Mass and perform other priestly duties. Despite defending himself bravely, David was proclaimed guilty and sentenced to death by Sir Robert Atkins. After bowing to the court, he was returned to prison.

After this, the condemned priest was brought to Newgate prison in London with John Kemble and questioned about the fictitious Oates Plot. However, Oates, Bedloe, Dugdale and Prance were unable to prove anything against him. Lord Shaftsbury advised him that if he gave some evidence about the plot or renounced his faith then his life would be saved and he would be greatly rewarded. However, as David said in his dying speech, "discover the plot I could not, for I knew of none; and conform I would not, for it was against my conscience." With that, he was returned to Usk and waited for three months for his call to death.

The call came on 27th August, 1679. Scolded for being too tolerant by the Privy Council, the local sheriff had to quickly find a gallows and an executioner after announcing the priest's immediate execution. However, all the town's carpenters hid, as well as the hangman, in an act of protest about the killing of the priest. In desperation, the sheriff bribed a convict to build the gallows with the promise of release. Thus, a rickety construction was hastily assembled but the convict, not being a specialist carpenter, did not build the gallows high enough for a man to hang from, so a ditch had to be dug below the noose. The wretched convict then had to run for his life after the local people threatened to stone him. For the sum of 12 crowns, the blacksmith was enticed to act as executioner. In the long term this was no gain though as he was afterwards shunned and his trade collapsed, leaving him to turn to thieving in an effort to survive.

After being drawn to the gallows at Usk, Monmouthshire, David made a lengthy speech to the assembled host:

*continues on page 96*

> *"I suffer not as a murderer, thief or such like malefactor, but as a Christian, and therefore am not ashamed."*

"Here is a numerous assembly - the great Saviour of the world save every soul of you all. I believe you are here met not only to see a fellow-native die, but also with expectation to hear a dying fellow-native speak. Let none of you suffer as a murderer, or a thief, but if as a Christian, let him not be ashamed (I St. Peter iv). I suffer not as a murderer, thief or such like malefactor, but as a Christian, and therefore am not ashamed."

He proceeded to tell the crowd how unjust was the charge against him contained in a vile pamphlet that claimed he had cheated a poor woman out of £30 under pretence of delivering her father's soul out of Purgatory. Moreover, he called God to witness that he never heard or knew anything about the Oates' Plot till public outrage had spread news of it across the country. In fact, no one could prove anything against him; he detested 'king-killing' and viewed it as opposite to the principles of the Catholic religion. To prove his loyalty he heartily prayed for the king. He then moved on to talking about the Catholic faith:

"My religion is the Roman Catholic; in it I have lived above these 40 years; in it I now die, and so fixedly die, that if all the good things in this world were offered me to renounce it, all should not remove me one hair's breadth from my Roman Catholic faith. A Roman Catholic I am; a Roman Catholic priest I am; a Roman Catholic priest of that religious Order called the Society of Jesus, I am; and I bless God who first called me, and I bless the hour in which I was first called both unto faith and function. Please now to observe, I was condemned for reading Mass, hearing confessions, administering the sacraments and so on. As for reading the Mass, it was the old, and still is the accustomed and laudable liturgy of the holy Church; and all the other acts, are acts of religion tending to the worship of God, and therefore dying for this I die for religion. And dying upon so good a score, as far as human frailty permits, I die with alacrity interior and exterior; from the abundance of the heart let not only mouths but faces also speak.

"Here, methinks, I feel flesh and blood ready to burst into loud cries - blood for blood, life for life. No, crieth holy gospel, forgive, and you shall be forgiven; pray for those that persecute you; love your enemies; and I profess myself as a child of the gospel, and the gospel I obey. Whomsoever present or absent I have ever offended, I humbly desire them to forgive me. As for my enemies, I freely forgive them all; my neighbours that betrayed me, the justices that committed me etc., but singularly and especially, I forgive my capital persecutor who hath long been thirsting after my blood [Arnold]; from my soul I forgive him, and wish his soul so well, that were it in my power, I would seat him a seraphim in heaven. Father, forgive them, they know not what they do.

"And with reason I love them also (my persecutors), for though they have done themselves a vast soul-prejudice, yet they have done me an incomparable favour, which I shall eternally acknowledge. But chiefly I love them for His sake, who said, love your enemies; and in testimony of my love, I wish them a good eternity. O eternity! eternity! how momentous are the glories, riches, and pleasures of this world? And how desirable art thou, O endless eternity? And for my said enemies attaining thereunto, I humbly beseech God to give them the grace of a true repentance, before they and this world part."

He then turned his attention to any Catholics who were present: "Friends, fear God, honour your king, be firm in your faith; avoid holy sin by frequenting the sacraments of holy Church. Patiently bear your persecutions and afflictions; forgive your enemies; your sufferings are great; I say, be firm in your faith to the end, yea even to death; then shall you heap unto yourselves celestial treasures in the heavenly Jerusalem, where no thief robbeth, no moth eateth, and no rust cometh. And have that blessed saying of St. Peter, prince of the apostles, always in your memory, which I heartily recommend to you, 'Let none of you suffer as a murderer or as a thief; but if as a Christian let him not be ashamed, but glorify God in his name'."

Having finished his speech, he applied himself to God with the following prayers:

"Sovereign Lord God, eternal Father of heaven, creator of all, conserver of all, sole author of grace and glory, with prostrate heart I adore Thee; and Thee only I adore as God. The giving of divine honour to any creature of highest degree, I abhor and detest as damnable idolatry. Incarnate Son of God, true God, Thou hast purchased a Church here on earth with Thy sacred blood, and planted it with Thy sacred labours; a Church, one holy Catholic and Apostolic; a Church to continue to the consummation of the world; whatever that Church of Thine hath by revelation from Thee, whatever that Church of Thine hath taught me, I believe it to an iota. God Holy Ghost, who maketh Thy sun to shine on good and bad, Thy rain to fall on the just and unjust, I praise Thy holy name, and thank thee for the innumerable benefits Thou hast been pleased to bestow and confer upon me, Thy unworthy servant, the 63 years I have now lived on earth. O Holy Trinity, three persons and one God, from the bottom of the heart I am sorry that ever I have offended Thee, my good God, even to an idle word; yet through Thy mercy, my God, and the merits of my Redeemer, I strongly hope for an eternal salvation. Sweet Jesus, receive my soul."

Finishing, David was at once executed, his feet dangling into the newly dug ditch. A local Protestant held the elderly Jesuit's hand throughout the ordeal, refusing to let go till the priest had died, thus ensuring that he could not be butchered whilst still alive and fully conscious. Finally, the dead body was cut down and spared the indignity of quartering, much to the relief of the majority of the crowd. He was later buried close to the entrance of the Anglican priory church in Usk.

## PRAYER TO THE MARTYRS FOR THE INCREASE OF PRIESTLY AND RELIGIOUS VOCATIONS

O God, who gave to our Blessed Martyrs a surpassing love of the Holy Mass: grant that, through their Intercession, our children may share the same love and generously accept the grace of vocation offered to so many. Through our Lord Jesus Christ.

R. Amen.

Con Appr. Eccl.
Nihil obstat - N. Ferraro,
Fidei Sub-Promotor Generalis.

**Note**

*Notification of favours etc. from the Forty Martyrs to be sent to Vice-Postulators, 31, Farm St., London, W. I.*

## THE FORTY MARTYRS OF ENGLAND AND WALES

### *Blessed*

John Houghton
Augustine Webster
Robert Lawrence
Richard Reynolds
John Stone
Cuthbert Mayne
Edmund Campion
Ralph Sherwin
Alexander Briant
John Paine
Luke Kirby
Richard Gwyn
Margaret Clitherow
Margaret Ward
Edmund Gennings
Swithun Wells
Eustace White
Polydore Plasden
John Boste
Robert Southwell

### *Blessed*

Henry Walpole
Philip Howard
John Jones
John Rigby
Anne Line
Nicholas Owen
Thomas Garnet
John Roberts
John Almond
Edmund Arrowsmith
Ambrose Barlow
Alban Roe
Henry Morse
John Southworth
John Plessington
Philip Evans
John Lloyd
John Wall
John Kemble
David Lewis

**FORTY MARTYRS, PRAY FOR US.**

## PRAYERS FOR THE CANONISATION OF FORTY MARTYRS OF ENGLAND AND WALES

THE PICTURE IS THE ALTARPIECE AT THE ENGLISH COLLEGE, ROME, BEFORE WHICH MANY OF THE ENGLISH AND WELSH MARTYRS PRAYED.

## PRAYERS FOR THEIR CANONISATION

I saw under the altar the souls of them that were slain for the Word of God and for the testimony which they held; and they cried with a loud voice, saying, How long, O Lord, holy and true, dost Thou not judge and vindicate our blood from them that dwell on the earth? (Apoc. 6)

V. Beneath the throne of God all the saints cry aloud.

R. Vindicate our blood, O Lord our God.

### *Let us pray.*

Grant, we beseech Thee, Almighty God, that we, who admire in Thy Martyrs the courage of their glorious confession, may witness in ourselves the power of their loving intercession.

O God, Who dost glorify those who glorify Thee, and Who art honoured in the honours of Thy saints, vouchsafe, we beseech Thee, by the solemn judgement of Thy Church to glorify the blood of the martyrs who have been put to death in England and Wales for the testimony of Jesus. Through the same Jesus Christ our Lord.

R. Amen.

**Our Father. Hail Mary. I believe in God.**

We grant an Indulgence of three hundred days for the devout recitation of the above prayers. (19 March 1960) William Card. Godfrey.

*Prayer card, believed to be from 1960, for the canonisation of the Forty Martyrs of England and Wales.*

PUBLISHED BY:
Gabriel Communications Ltd. 1st Floor, St James's Buildings, Oxford Street, Manchester M1 6FP.
Tel: 0161 236 8856   Fax: 0161 237 4381   Web: www.totalcatholic.com

WORDS & RESEARCH:
JAMES KELLY

DESIGN & PRODUCTION:
BRENDAN GILLIGAN

PRINTED BY:
Buxton Press Limited, Palace Road, Buxton, Derbyshire, SK17 6AE.

ISBN 1-904657-19-2
barcode.co.uk
9 781904 657194